T0288029

Pickleball for Life

Prevent Injury, Play Your Best & Enjoy the Game

Jes Reynolds

Sanjay Saint, MD, MPH

Published in the United States of America by
Michigan Publishing
Manufactured in the United States of America

ISBN 978-1-60785-732-7 (paper)
ISBN 978-1-60785-733-4 (e-book)

An imprint of Michigan Publishing, Michigan Publishing Services
serves the publishing needs of the University of Michigan community
by making high-quality scholarship widely available in print and
online. It represents a new model for authors seeking to share their
work within and beyond the academy, offering streamlined selection,
production, and distribution processes. Michigan Publishing Services
is intended as a complement to more formal modes of publication in
a wide range of disciplinary areas.
https://www.fulcrum.org/mps

To my teammates in sport, fitness, and life.
We've run a thousand miles and played a
million games . . . and now this.

—Jes Reynolds

To my extended family and to my pickle
pals.

—Sanjay Saint

Contents

About the Authors   vii

Acknowledgments   ix

Preface   xi

Part 1: The Basics   1
Story from the Court: Greg Tighe

1. Introduction   5
2. Finding Joy in Pickleball   11
3. Meet Your Trainer   25
4. Wellness Habits for Longevity   32
5. Crafting Your Own Fitness & Nutrition Plan   40
6. Nutrition 101   46

Part 2: Train to Be a Better Player   57
Story from the Court: Eliza Stein

7. Core & Posture   61
8. Mobility & Flexibility   83
9. Balance, Coordination & Agility   102

Part 3: Prevent & Manage Injuries   115
Story from the Court: Julie Muer

10. Improving Upper Body Mobility & Preventing
Neck, Shoulder, and Elbow Problems   120

11. Improving Hip Mobility & Preventing
   Lower Back Problems   141
12. Preventing Hamstring, Quadriceps, IT Band
   & Knee Problems   160
13. Preventing Calf, Achilles, and Ankle Problems
   & Managing Plantar Fasciitis   175
14. Preventing Falls & Eye Injuries   187

Part 4: Pre- and Postgame
Routines & Recovery   199
   Story from the Court: Mark Kielb
15. Pregame Warm-Up Routines   204
16. Postgame Stretch Routine   218
17. Sanjay's Pickleball Equipment Cabinet   224

   Appendix: Foam Rolling Guide   235
   References   243
   Index   249

DISCLAIMER: The content of this book is for informational purposes only and is not intended to diagnose, treat, cure, or guarantee prevention of any condition, disease, or injury. Please seek advice from your health care provider for your personal health concerns before undertaking a new health care regimen.

About the Authors

Jes Reynolds is the owner and fitness coach at Elevate Fitness in Ann Arbor, Michigan. She earned her bachelor of science degree in kinesiology from Michigan State University and has several additional certifications. Jes developed "The Lean Code" program, which teaches people how to eat, train, and live lean so they can stay athletic and fit throughout every phase of life. Her passion for athletics and competing began at an early age and led her to personal training and coaching. Jes works with people of all ages and abilities, from college athletes, former professional athletes, and Olympians to those with physical disabilities.

Sanjay Saint, MD, MPH, is the Chief of Medicine at the VA Ann Arbor Healthcare System, the George Dock Professor of Internal Medicine at the University of Michigan, and an avid pickleball player. In addition to numerous biomedical publications, Dr. Saint has written for *The Wall Street Journal* and *Harvard Business Review* and  has coauthored several books published by Oxford University Press, including *Preventing Hospital Infections*, *Teaching Inpatient Medicine: What Every Physician Needs to Know*, and *The Saint-Chopra Guide to Inpatient Medicine (4th Edition)*. He also coauthored two books published by the University of Michigan: *Thirty Rules for Healthcare Leaders* and *The Mentoring Guide: Helping Mentors and Mentees Succeed*. He lives, works, and plays in Ann Arbor, Michigan.

Acknowledgments

Jes would like to thank each and every one of her clients and members for motivating her to continue learning and growing as a trainer and teacher. Jes also extends tremendous gratitude to her awesome, close-knit circle of friends—her "ohana." She feels fortunate to compete, laugh, and have the most important conversations with Rebekah, Randi, Julie, Lindsay, Stacia, Autumn, Sarah, Kusull, and especially, her mom: thank you for your amazing friendship and consistent support. Chris Johnson deserves a special shout-out as he, unknowingly, instilled the value that trainers can have a larger vision, one that truly makes a difference in people's lives.

Sanjay would like to thank the Stein family (Steve, Lori, Bennett, Allie, and Eliza) for introducing him to this addictive game. Sanjay is also extremely grateful to his pickle pals for being so welcoming both on and off the court. Special thanks to Asif Amin, Michael Barton, Tim Berla, Franklin Bradley, Gerald Caddel, Susan Canizares, Phil Campbell, Colette Donaldson-Massoglia, Emily Douglas, Charles Eveler, Charles Fahlsing, Brian Grant, Kevin Harding, John Hostetler, Christy Howden, Joe Ingersoll, Mark Kielb, Rex Lau, Dave Lloyd, Jim Marshall, David Massoglia, Evan Meili, Gordie Morris, Ian Moss, Partha Mukhopadhyay, Rishi Narayan, Kate Peterson,

Pedja Rakic, Jim Richter, Martha Rogers Stange, Jim Sterken, Jim Swendris, Greg Tighe, Gonzalo Ubillus, Tony Werstein, Dorothy West, Leslie White, and Helen Wo (with shout-outs to Greg Tighe for so graciously organizing our games and Jim Richter for use of his "speakeasy" court). Finally, a special thanks to Veronica Saint for keeping the kitchen open late on pickleball nights and to Sean and Kirin Saint for enthusiastically embracing this terrific game.

Both Jes and Sanjay are grateful to Jennifer Berry for her wonderful editing and to Greg Tighe, Mark Kielb, Julie Muer, and Eliza Stein for their personal contributions to the book. This book could not have been accomplished without the diligence, persistence, and superb coordination of Rachel Ehrlinger—we appreciate her commitment to excellence and her patience throughout.

Preface

My name is Sanjay and I am addicted to pickleball. ☺

I was introduced to the game in 2019, and I've been hooked ever since. From the beginning, I've enjoyed the fast play, the short learning curve, the teamwork required in doubles, and the welcoming attitudes of other players.

As a former tennis player, I appreciate that I no longer have to serve overhand or cover a large amount of the court. The camaraderie among players is also notable. Most of them seem to be happy just playing and smashing the whiffle ball back and forth. I enjoy the "in-the-moment" feel of the game and even the sound of the paddle touching the ball. There is something mesmerizing about that "pop-pop-pop," I must admit.

Something else that struck me when I began was the demographics of the players. Tennis is largely skewed toward those who are young, athletic, and very mobile. Not so with pickleball. I played at a local recreation center, where the average player was over 60 years old. At age 56, I was one of the younger players.

The pickleballers I met came in all sizes and shapes and had a wide range of physical abilities. Some were in terrific shape, but this was the exception. I came to realize that several players I met had battled conditions like cancer or stroke. Pickleball was their preferred source of exercise and engagement with others.

Given these demographics, I wasn't surprised to find that players often got injured—myself included. It wasn't long before I was hit with plantar fasciitis, shoulder pain, Achilles soreness, hamstring problems, iliotibial (IT) band issues, and other injuries I have since forgotten about.

I also observed injuries in opponents and friends—two of whom experienced Achilles tears. Another player fell on an outstretched arm and broke a bone in his hand. I have also seen players pulling up in the middle of a game due to pulled hamstrings and groins, as well as back injuries. And this is on top of the players I know who must manage chronic ailments like shoulder pain or "tennis elbow" or hip issues.

I tried to play through my pain and injuries with the help of anti-inflammatory drugs and ice wraps. But I soon realized that popping pills after each pickleball outing was not a smart long-term strategy.

I set out to learn how to improve my balance, nutrition, mobility, and flexibility so I could play without pain and medications. I knew that eventually the medications would stop working or cause side effects like stomach ulcers. I also knew that I would keep playing even if it hurt. Remember, I am addicted to the game. ☺

So I got help. I told my awesome trainer, Jes Reynolds, about the pickleball injuries that plagued my friends and me. Her guidance was game-changing. She guided me through flexibility training and ways to improve my nutrition and core strength. She taught me miniexercises I could do throughout the day to help with my shoulder and ankle mobility. Since her expertise has helped me, I thought she would be the perfect person to lead this book.

Combining Jes's vast knowledge as a trainer with my love of the game, we wrote this book to help other pickle-ballers avoid injury and continue to play this game for a very long time. But we know that watching a visual demonstration is often better than reading words on a page. That's why we've included links to videos, led by Jes, that will guide you through these exercises.

We've also included helpful pictures and drawings. Our illustrator, Victoria Bornstein, did a lovely job capturing the complexity of the human body in a creative yet simple-to-understand manner. Finally, each section features a "story from the court" told by pickleballers from around the country. These glimpses into pickleballers' lives remind us why we love this sport.

My goal is to play until I am 100 years old. Will you join me?

Sanjay Saint, MD, MPH
Ann Arbor, MI

PART 1
The Basics

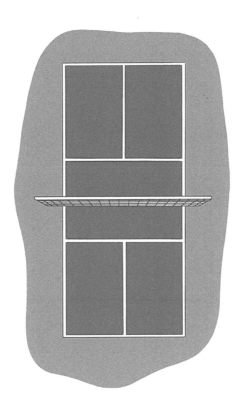

Story from the Court

One Sunday afternoon, I was playing pickleball with a group I organize. John, a member of my group, entered the courts carrying a strange-looking wheelchair. The wheels were larger than normal and were mounted at a different angle than most.

Following behind John was another man seated in a conventional-looking wheelchair. John introduced us to his friend, who was named Kenny. He and John went out to an open court and set up to play. Kenny transferred to the other wheelchair, which was his preferred chair for playing pickleball.

Kenny had only played pickleball four times before but came to the courts to see if anyone would play with him. I was sitting on the sidelines at the time watching a nearby game. Once that game ended, I asked Haley, a fellow player, if she would play with John, Kenny, and me. Haley happily agreed.

We played three games, each time changing partners. We asked Kenny if there were any special rules that applied to him. He said the only difference was that he could allow the ball to bounce up to two times before returning it. John got mixed up on this during one rally, stopping play after Kenny let the ball bounce twice before striking it. Whoops!

But it was all in good fun. For it only being his fifth time playing pickleball, Kenny played very well! John recovered from his embarrassment too. I had to leave after the third game but heard that the group invited Kenny to join them for more games. I was really glad to hear that.

—Greg Tighe, Ypsilanti, MI

Part 1: The Basics

Many people wish they had more time to dedicate to their fitness, nutrition, and the activities that bring them joy. If you've picked up this book, chances are you've found a hint of that joy in playing this addictive game with the silly name.

For centuries, athletics has been an enjoyable means of exercise and a way for humans to bond with one another. Unfortunately, many of us often choose not to join in the fun, fearing we are too out of shape or not skilled enough. Luckily, as you've already read and will hear more of in the chapters ahead, pickleball is a sport for all ages, all skill levels, and all abilities.

In this section, we will coach you through the basics of your pickleball journey. You'll meet your new personal trainer, Jes, and learn small things you can do to improve your nutrition. You'll also come up with your own fitness goals and be mindful while doing so. All these things impact your game!

You can form daily habits to improve your fitness and nutrition in the simplest of tasks. These next six chapters will introduce you to the key components of playing pickleball for life, and you may just learn something new about this sport you've come to love. We'll also share the joy that we and others have experienced while playing and why we keep returning to the court.

1

Introduction

Pickleball is the fastest-growing sport in the country. That is quite a feat, since the name *pickleball* sounds less like a sport and more like something you might order at a new age deli. In just a few decades, it's established its own national association and tournament—not to mention the many regional clubs and tourneys—for all ages and skill brackets.

Many people choose pickleball over tennis because it's less physically demanding. A pickleball court is smaller, and you usually play doubles rather than singles. For these reasons, it's become popular with older adults. A recent *New York Post* article interviewed physical therapist Roland Rodriguez, who stated, "A common theme with this population is that they play every day. They describe themselves as obsessed and many injuries are from repeated stress." The article states, "Pickleball is to blame for most of the sports injuries in his older patients." Yet "mature competitors shouldn't ditch it. They should just play smarter. Rodriguez advises dynamic stretching and warm ups, balance and stability exercises along with cross training and simply listening to one's body."[1]

But pickleball isn't just for those over 50. The sport has grown in popularity with younger people, with the average age of casual players now being 33.6 years.[2] The sport even made a recent feature in the pop culture magazine *Vanity Fair*. Celebrities like Leonardo DiCaprio, Melinda Gates, Brené Brown, and others have embraced the game.[3,4] Unlike many other sports, pickleball appeals to a wide range of individuals.[5] It's "accessible, affordable, and allows an almost unparalleled competitive balance across generations and genders."[3]

During the first year of the COVID-19 pandemic, the number of pickleball players grew by 21.3 percent. This was more than double its growth from the previous three years.[2] It's low impact, so many people assume it will be an easy sport to pick up. However, players' bursts of high-intensity efforts in the game often lead to injuries.

Before we dive into the crux of this book, let's take a walk through the history of pickleball. Sources for this history include usapickleball.org and the *Seattle Times* article, "Pickleball Began on Bainbridge Island in 1965 as a Summertime Diversion for Bored Kids and Since Has Ballooned into a Full-Fledged Sport for All Ages."[6,7]

Brief History of Pickleball

On a summer evening in 1965, US politician Joel Pritchard and his friend, businessman Bill Bell, had just finished a day of golfing. They returned to the Pritchards' home in Bainbridge Island, Washington, to find their families bored out of their minds.

Joel and Bill decided to find a way for the children to entertain themselves and leave the adults in peace. The Pritchards had a badminton court but lacked the proper equipment to play a full game. So the men gathered ping-pong and paddleball paddles and a perforated plastic ball they had on hand. They sent the children to the court with the mishmash of equipment, hoping for the best. Later, they returned to find the children having a grand time.

We don't know for sure where the name *pickleball* came from. The most convincing story (at least to us) says the game is named after the Pritchard family's cocker spaniel, Pickles. The dog was notorious for chasing the plastic ball and running off with it.

Throughout that first weekend, as various friends and family began to play, the game began to take shape. At first, they left the badminton net at its typical height of 60 inches. After a bit of experimenting, they lowered the net to 34 inches—two inches below tennis height.

The next weekend, the families met up again and invited their friend Barney McCallum. Together, the three men developed a formal set of rules for the new game, based heavily on badminton scoring. Among them were the seven-foot exclusion zone—an area from which a player cannot make a shot—and a requirement to serve underhand. A player scores when the opposing side fails to return the ball. The shot must bounce once before being fielded by the opposing player.

As they defined their new game, the men kept the focus on their original goal. They wanted something everyone in the family could enjoy *together*, regardless of age, physical limitations, or conditioning.

In 1967, Joel's neighbor, Bob O'Brian, built the first permanent pickleball court in his backyard. Through the 1970s, pickleball became ensconced within a new organization. In 1984, a group of players formed the United States Amateur Pickleball Association (USAPA) to shepherd the sport forward. The USAPA published the first rulebook that same year, accelerating the sport's nationwide growth. By 1990, pickleball was played in all 50 US states.

By the turn of the millennium, the largest tournaments featured about 100 players. The number grew to almost 300 in 2003, and in 2005, the USAPA transformed into the USA Pickleball Association (still known as USAPA). It gained a new board of directors, nonprofit status, and a consolidated database of places to play the game (via an associated website).[8]

In 2008, the game was included in National Senior Games Association events. That year also saw the first mass media coverage of the sport, including being featured in a brief segment on the ABC program *Good Morning America*.

The game truly came into its own when in 2009, the USAPA hosted its first national tournament. By 2013, there were more than 4,000 USAPA members, which grew to 10,000 by 2015. That year, one sports industry association estimated some two million people played the sport, with 12,800 courts in the US!

The last of the three original founders of the game, Barney McCallum, passed away in 2019. The next year, the

USAPA had grown to over 40,000 members and renamed itself "USA Pickleball."[9] According to the most recent estimates, 4.8 million people in the US currently play pickleball.[10]

Pickleball also appeals to people who previously played other racquet sports, like tennis. In Kennewick, Washington, cardiologist Ken Curry was a college tennis player who made it to the 1978 qualifying round of the Australian Open. Dr. Curry had always looked down his nose at pickleball, though. "I thought it was a geezer sport," he admitted in a *Wall Street Journal* article. But Dr. Curry's brother finally convinced the cardiologist to give the game a shot. "After one game, I was hooked," Dr. Curry said.[11]

The game has grown into a family affair for the Currys. Two of Dr. Curry's children play pickleball at high levels, and his son-in-law won gold at the Australian Pickleball Nationals in 2018. Even Dr. Curry's wife, Patty—who had been driven away from tennis by her husband's intense training—thoroughly enjoys the game. Dr. Curry is quite committed to the game, practicing and playing up to four days a week for two to three hours at a time.

But perhaps pickleball's growth and wide appeal aren't just about physical fitness. The sport is less directly competitive than most others, so it often has a relaxing effect. Many players report that it lowers stress and anxiety and produces feelings of joy. Couldn't we all use more joy in this day and age? But more on this in the next chapter.

Take-Home Points

1. Pickleball was created to be an accessible game that people of every age and skill level can enjoy.

2. The sport is growing rapidly—look around you to see what clubs, teams, or groups are in your community!

3. While pickleball is intended for all players, remember that putting your health first will always benefit you.

2

Finding Joy in Pickleball

The "Story from the Court" by Greg Tighe is the type of feel-good story most of us love reading about. Pickleball is full of such stories and experiences, as we will discuss in this chapter, which focuses on *why* so many of us love this game with the ridiculous name.

Speaking for myself (Sanjay here), I had to do some soul-searching to discover why I enjoy pickleball. To begin with, I believe meeting our needs leads to happiness and fulfillment. Professional success feels good, but it doesn't fill all needs. Simply put, success is not the only thing that makes a person happy (and it sometimes doesn't lead to much happiness at all).

Pickleball, on the other hand, represents togetherness, play, laughter, and healthy competition. I appreciate a meritocracy—but not from a cutthroat perspective. The better player or team should win, and in pickleball, that usually happens. There is a sense of competition on the court, but it is accompanied by a spirit of collaboration and companionship. Camaraderie is formed.

In pickleball, players often switch partners regularly. This is contrary to tennis, a similar sport, where you often play singles or with the same doubles partner. I've partnered with people of all skill levels, each game different than the last.

For me, pickleball is a reminder that it doesn't matter what our titles are, what kinds of cars we drive, or what the sizes of our homes are. In the end, we are all human beings. And yes, the better pickleballer should win, but their value as a human is not dependent on that. This constant realization makes me happy.

We suspect that most people play pickleball because it brings them joy. With this in mind, let's learn how pickleball is making its way to surprising places. Next, we'll discuss the science and literature behind concepts such as joy and happiness and tie these concepts back to pickleball.

Inmate Pickleball

The unprecedented growth of pickleball has culminated in a sort of renaissance for the sport as it expands into new venues. Over the last few years, pickleball has been named the fastest-growing sport in the US, and it has made its way into unexpected areas.[1]

"When you're on the court, you can't think of anything else other than hitting the ball over the net," said Roger BelAir, a financial expert, author, public speaker, and pickleball guru from Seattle.[2] In 2018, Mr. BelAir donated pickleball equipment to the Cook County Jail in Chicago.[2,3] His purpose in donating? To provide a relaxing activity and increase camaraderie among inmates.

It took time for the inmates to adjust to the idea. But once they got into the game, 19-year-old Alberto Manzo says, "[It] made everybody bring out their inner child."[2] If for only an hour, the sport allows these inmates to escape the hard reality of their circumstances. One could say it even brings them a glimmer of hope.

Most jails in the US do not need programs for physical and mental fitness. Usually, jails are short-stay areas for people in the criminal justice system awaiting their trials. However, Cook County is unusual. It has a population that's large and that stays in its system for years—sometimes as many as 10 years—waiting for their trials to move forward.

Cook County Jail saw a need to introduce programs to better enable these inmates to try to change their lives. So the jail worked with Mr. BelAir to give the inmates a new activity. Of course, it's a privilege in the jail, not a right. The ability to play pickleball must be earned through good behavior and avoiding disciplinary incidents.

Unlike other sports offered in jails and prisons, pickle-ball is more about enjoying the game rather than competition and winning. "The most popular sport on the inside is basketball," says Mr. BelAir. "But you have young, aggressive men. And, as you can imagine, once they get on the court, there's a lot of injuries. There's some people that even want to eliminate basketball from being played on the inside."[4] With pickleball, the game is indeed fun, but it can also lower baseline anxiety in a population with few mental health escapes.

And for many of us, pickleball is very much an escape. It's really hard to think of anything else when you are hitting the ball! And if you're daydreaming and the ball hits you in the chest or whizzes by you, your partner will likely kindly remind you to get your head in the game. ☺ In short, pickleball requires players to be fully present, all in, engaged. One could almost say it requires us to be mindful.

Many activities, of course, can help us become more mindful. Examples are taking a walk in nature, playing a musical instrument, listening to music, praying, meditating—and, we propose, playing a game of pickleball. Mindfulness is defined as "the awareness that arises by paying attention on purpose, in the present moment, non-judgmentally."[5]

As a doctor who truly cares about the well-being of his patients, I know how valuable mindfulness can be for them, their families, and the physicians attending to them. Mindfulness gives everyone the opportunity to address and reduce the internalized stress of difficult or frightening medical situations. It gives you the ability to sit with challenges without reaction, blame, or apathy. Instead, we can have true respect for one another as patients, family members, doctors, and colleagues. This is an invaluable asset to have when a person's physical health is at stake.

Our first attempt to include mindfulness in our health care system utilized a systematic review led by nurse scientist Dr. Heather Gilmartin. The review found that brief mindfulness interventions may improve health care workers' well-being.[6] Note that *brief* is defined relatively here; it's four hours or less of mindfulness training. We wanted to bring the benefits of mindfulness to physician-patient interactions. But we also knew the challenge busy providers would face dedicating significant amounts of their time to being mindful.

Then we thought, "Well, what if we tied hand hygiene—something that we do *multiple* times a day, and even more now with COVID—to a moment of mindfulness?" In short, every time we wash our hands, we do it mind*fully* rather than mind*less*ly.

We thus conducted a randomized trial that focused on medical trainees and attending physicians. They watched Andy Puddicombe's TED Talk on mindfulness.[7] Then they participated in a guided discussion on using mindfulness to enhance safety in the hospital.[8] We found that hand hygiene adherence rates improved significantly after this simple intervention.

For me (Sanjay), the typical experience with this begins when I put my hand below the automatic hand sanitizer dispenser before entering a patient's room. Before the intervention, I might have been thinking, "Oh, I've just got to get through this handwashing thing." But now, I actually take time to feel the hand sanitizer, notice its smell, notice the fact that it is evaporating. And for me, it's a cue to be fully present when I interact with my patient.

This may be one of a dozen interactions that I am going to have with a patient and their family that day. But for that patient, those next 15 minutes when I sit down and talk with them are arguably the most important 15 minutes of their day. You can see this by the reaction when I enter the room. They may be on the phone, but when I come in, they say, "Doctor is here. I'll call you back. Bye, love ya." And that's quite remarkable!

The mindful moment outside the room is a reminder to me that I've got to be on, fully engaged, and completely present, because the stakes are high. I am about to connect with another human about their health. They are often feeling vulnerable and frightened. This is when I will let them know, for example, what the CT scan revealed or when they can go home. The sad truth is that I often see patients and families on the worst days of their lives—when they are frightened, anxious, distraught, and without hope. Being mindful and fully present allows me to connect with them on a human-to-human level. Mindfulness helps me comfort them and, hopefully, help them feel better.

Knowing that mindfulness can reduce stress, increase focus, and help you connect with those around you, why not try to play pickleball more mindfully? How would you do that? By noticing the wind or the sound of the ball as it strikes your opponent's paddle, the sound of it striking yours, where the ball bounces, the sound of the ball hitting the ground, and the sounds all around. By looking your opponents in the eye and thanking them for a fun game. By encouraging your partner after a good shot or a missed one—and doing it while you are fully present.

The simple act of being more present during a game and grateful for the opportunity to play will likely increase the amount of joy that you get from playing this game with the funny name.[9]

Happiness versus Joy

Most of us seek joy and happiness in our lives, which begs the question: Is joy the same thing as happiness? And even more to the point, can we find either of these anymore? Especially living in a postpandemic world, social unrest is only a TV news report away.

Let's start with some basic definitions to clarify what we are talking about. The *Oxford English Dictionary* (*OED*) defines joy as "the feeling . . . of being highly pleased or delighted."[10] It defines happiness as the "state of pleasurable content-ment of the mind."[11] Some may have learned these terms as meaning the opposite of how they are defined here. But for the purposes of this book, we will consider happiness to be more enduring and joy to be more fleeting. Regardless of how you use the terms, the end goal is the same: to attain lasting, deep satisfaction in one's life. Stringing together enough moments of joy may do just that.

You see, happiness may be hard to quantify, but joy is everywhere! There are books on joy, podcasts on joy. In fact, you can go to IKEA, pay $7.90, and purportedly find joy in a small home furnishing. There are, in short, a huge variety of products and services on offer to bring you fleeting joy.

Laura Holson asked in a *New York Times* piece, "If joy is everywhere, why does happiness feel so elusive?"[12] Given the rates of depression, anxiety, and suicidality we have in this country, Ms. Holson is really asking: Are we actually living in a *posthappiness world*? She quotes Dr. Dacher Keltner from the University of California at Berkeley: "Something else is making happiness harder to attain: a lack of togetherness." Holson explains, "[Keltner] pointed to churches and other religious congregations, which have historically been central to a community's integrity. 'Church gave you awe, joy, ecstasy,' Dr. Keltner said. 'You collected in a group. You sang a little. You gave money. You got to chant.'" Ms. Holson wrote this piece months before COVID-19 hit the United States. Restrictions to stem the repeated surges of COVID-19 have exacerbated a systemic kind of isolation in our society.

Ingrid Fetell Lee wrote a book entitled *Joyful*, in which she writes, "Joy isn't something we just find. It's also something we can make, for ourselves and for those around us."[13] This is a crucial point: *joy is in our control*. It is something that we can *do*. When interviewed, Ms. Fetell Lee said, "I don't think about happiness anymore. I think about joy. And if you string together enough moments of joy, maybe you can have a happy life."[12]

Another terrific book that addresses joy is named, fittingly enough, *The Book of Joy*, by the Dalai Lama and Archbishop Desmond Tutu.[14] The Dalai Lama wrote, "Everyone seeks happiness, joyfulness, but from the outside—from money, from power, from big car, from big house. Most people never pay much attention to the ultimate source of a happy life, which is inside, not outside." Taken together, *Joyful* and *The Book of Joy* tell us three things:

1. joy is attainable,

2. joy is under our control, and

3. joy comes from within.

Experiencing Joy

In *The Book of Joy*, Archbishop Tutu and the Dalai Lama list three key factors that can help increase a person's sense of joy.[14] The first is our ability to reframe a given situation in a more positive way. Next is our ability to experience gratitude and to be thankful for what we have. Finally, it is our choice to be kind and generous. Note that for all three of these factors, it's on us. It is within our ability—and it is *our* choice—to reach for joy.

Desmond Tutu writes, "Compassion and generosity are not just lofty virtues—they are at the center of our humanity, which makes our lives joyful and meaningful."[14] (As discussed more in the following section, that is certainly my experience with pickleball! Most of the people I've played with and against are kind and generous people interested in connecting.)

Psychologist Rick Hanson has talked and written extensively about how we can "hardwire" processes into the brain to help us become happy.[15] Dr. Hanson says humans tend to focus on the negative because it has conferred an evolutionary advantage in the past.

Imagine a person with a positivity bias looking out their kitchen window when a rabbit happily hops across their yard. They might pause their dishwashing to observe the cute rabbit and take joy from the simple beauty of the moment. If, however, that person had a negativity bias, they might assume that the rabbit was trying to escape from a predator. Suddenly, the sympathetic nervous system kicks in, and they begin searching for danger. Could that be a lion behind that bush?

Evolutionarily speaking, this person with a negativity bias was the one who survived. The one who simply enjoyed the bunny in their yard wouldn't have survived the one-in-a-thousand chance that there actually was a carnivore sneaking up from behind the bush.

I do a lot of teaching at the University of Michigan, which means that I receive a lot of teaching evaluations. Suppose I get 10 of them from my trainees: nine of them are good, but one of them isn't so good. Later, that negative evaluation is the one I'm talking about with my wife—who happens to be a psychotherapist, which comes in handy! It's the negative evaluation that I'm thinking about before I go to bed. That's the one I'm thinking about when I wake up early in the morning, and that's the one that will bum me out a bit.

We pay attention to the negative because of our built-in negativity bias. The good news is, though, that we can overcome this bias—and one way is through kindness.

Elizabeth Bernstein, a terrific writer at *The Wall Street Journal*, talks about the benefits of being kind. She cites data that show being kind to others lowers stress hormone levels and diminishes negative thoughts and so increases our happiness. Bernstein says kindness also fosters improved connections with others.[16] All these positive benefits are crucially important.

Bernstein is not the only one to hold such a perspective. "The key to our success is not the survival of the fittest," Bernstein says, quoting Jamil Zaki, Stanford psychologist. "It's the survival of the friendliest." Sara Konrath from Indiana University is also quoted, saying, "Kindness is a lifestyle."[16] Like any lifestyle, kindness is a choice we can make.

Being Kinder Every Day

Flight attendants tell passengers that if there is a loss of cabin pressure, they should put the oxygen mask on themselves before assisting others. Similarly, to be kind to others, we must first cultivate kindness for ourselves. Being kind to ourselves is necessary self-care, and we're finding that this is even more true now than it ever has been. Be mindful of not getting too down on yourself if you're playing poorly or miss a clear winner at the net.

Like mindfulness, kindness need not be a grand undertaking. It can be as simple as a heartfelt "I really enjoyed playing with you" to your partner after a game. Or not getting visibly annoyed at your partner for missing an easy point.

Let me give you an example of an act of kindness that I witnessed while playing pickup pickleball at our rec center in Ann Arbor. Every time I think of it, I feel joyful and appreciative—one more joyful moment I can string together with many others.

Let me set the scene. Next to each court, there is a box where people who are waiting can place their paddles for the next game. If there are four people waiting, four paddles go in the box.

One day, as I waited with my three friends for our chance to play, I saw my buddy Tony. He was waiting at the court next to mine. But with only three paddles in Tony's box, he and his coplayers had room for one more.

One of the regular players came by looking for a box to throw his paddle in. Let's call him Bob. Bob was an older man with several medical issues, and he struggled to play the game. He noticed that the box for Tony's court held only three paddles, so he asked Tony who else was waiting with him.

Tony listed the other players. Bob said they were much better than him, and he didn't want to waste their time by playing with them. Tony knew this would be the case for nearly every court, so he said, "Hey, Bob, how about if you and I partner up?"

Bob, visibly relieved, replied, "Really? You sure? I'm not that good."

Tony replied, "You're good enough, and I would love to play with you."

As I witnessed this, I felt great admiration for Tony. He did something that I likely would not have done. (I would like to think I would have been this gracious, but I would be deluding myself.) I told Tony afterward how impressed I was with his generosity. He said that he and Bob were beaten pretty badly, but he enjoyed the game anyway.

Then COVID-19 hit, and I didn't see Tony or Bob for months. Tony's actions that day took on new meaning for me when, a few weeks later, we received an email from Bob's wife. She wrote to inform the Ann Arbor pickleball community that Bob had passed away peacefully. She told us how appreciative Bob was of all the people who played pickleball with him during the final years of his life while his health was declining.

The kindness I saw from Tony that day has changed how I view being someone's partner. It was a little thing to Tony, but it likely was the last time Bob ever played. I like to think he felt included and wanted on the court.

Daniel Pink wrote in his book *Drive*, "We know that the richest experiences in our lives aren't when we are clamoring for validation from others, but when we are listening to our own voice—doing something that matters, doing it well, and doing it in the service of a cause larger than ourselves."[17] What he's talking about is *meaning* and *purpose.*

In the graduation speech he gave at the University of North Carolina at Chapel Hill in 2014, Dr. Atul Gawande said, "The search for purpose is really a search for a place, not an idea. It is a search for a location in the world where you want to be part of making things better for others in your own small way."[18]

For many of us, that place is our regular pickleball venue with our pickle pals. We are the lucky ones.

Take-Home Points

1. Be mindful when you step out onto the pickleball court. Listen to the footsteps on the court, and feel the ball hitting your paddle. This just may improve your well-being.

2. Being joyful is a conscious decision, and it doesn't come from outward things.

3. Invite people to play with you. Being kind goes a long way, and it could mean the world to that person.

3

Meet Your Trainer

Hello! My name is Jes. Nice to meet you! Starting today, I'm planning to take control of all your nutrition, fitness, and injury prevention choices for the rest of your life. I'm just kidding . . . kind of. But from here until the end of this book, I will be your personal trainer.

As much as I wish I could wave a wand to get you fit, it's you—and only you—that can do this. You determine your fitness, nutrition, and long-term health destiny (at least the parts that are influenced by your choices). But as a trainer, it is my goal to empower you to take charge of your health and realize your true potential. This means I might get a little bossy sometimes! ☺

Sure, there's a chance my bossiness won't be enough to transform your fitness habits. That's OK! I'm betting that your love for pickleball will help with that. You see, I've got something on you pickleball players. Some might call it an "ace in the hole."

I know how passionate you are about pickleball. I know it brings you joy, and I know you want to play pickleball for life. These are the secret weapons that I, as a trainer, can use to motivate you into better health choices.

In the world today, joy and passion can often be quite fleeting. When you find something that consistently brings both, it motivates and inspires you to do better. And I hope the stories and information in these pages will do just that for you.

Creating Consistent Habits

I believe the first step to long-term fitness and well-being is creating consistent habits. Since I entered the fitness industry, I've been obsessed with finding the best result-producing system that anyone can follow. Over time, I've developed techniques designed to maximize your fitness level and nutrition intake to help you become the healthiest version of yourself.

I've spent years refining my system. I've used myself as a human guinea pig. I've read hundreds of books and thousands of articles and attended more certification seminars than I can count. Through these efforts, I've designed a proven process for maintaining a great physique, awesome nutrition, and amazing performance at any age.

I'm so glad you're here, because I want you to learn the system. You can use it to become a fitter, healthier, and more athletic pickleballer. My hope is that you'll see how consistent habits translate into joyfully pursuing your passion for pickleball—for life.

Getting fitter, healthier, and more athletic means making some lifestyle changes. Change doesn't always come easily—even with passion, joy, motivation, a proven system, and a bossy trainer!

Sometimes you need a personal epiphany or an "aha" moment to shift your perspective and do things differently. As you read through this book, I encourage you to keep your mind open and ready for an "aha" moment. It will inspire you to take your health and fitness habits to the next level.

Finding a Goal

"I want the same physique as Cristiano Ronaldo."

That's what Sanjay told me the first day we met.

"OK . . . ," I said. I wondered if he knew this would take significant time and effort—and a much larger home workout room. Despite my inner monologue, which I did not share with him, we made a plan and started to execute it.

As the weeks wore on and my demands on Sanjay grew, I sensed what I like to call "zombie client syndrome." It's common with smart, strong-willed people like Sanjay.

Zombie client syndrome presents as someone who is listening and engaged. The person knows exactly how to answer when you ask a question. But if you offer a suggestion related to their goal, they're not listening. They've "zombied out" and will not take the necessary steps to reach their goal.

People with zombie client syndrome haven't admitted to themselves that they don't really want to do what you are asking. So you have to dig a little deeper. You must observe how they react to coaching, ask questions, and find just the right teachable moment. And when you find that moment, it's the open door for things to really change.

In Sanjay's case, we had two such moments. The first happened when Sanjay was helping me brainstorm ways to get my program down on paper. I told him one example goal of my program.

"You should plan to live to be 100," I said.

The lightbulb came on!

Somehow, I'd done it. I'd broken through the tough surface that we call "Dr. Saint" and found a goal that motivated and intrigued Sanjay. He had walked through the door and the zombie retreated!

After that moment, I knew we had turned the tide. We were no longer focused on an unrealistic surface goal. We had set a course toward something truly worth achieving: a positive vision of longevity. A vision in which you assume the best—living to 100—instead of the worst. One in which you find joy in realizing the best version of yourself in health and fitness instead of emulating someone else. One in which you make the best choices you can to stay strong, healthy, active, and fit for as long as you can.

And then he found pickleball.

Achieving Your Vision

I didn't see the pickleball thing coming. One day we were talking about spikeball, music, current events, and spirituality. Then suddenly, we only talked about pickleball.

"My friend tore his Achilles playing pickleball. What would cause this, Jes?" Sanjay asked.

"Another friend tore his Achilles playing pickleball, and I saw it happen. What is going on with people getting injured like this, Jes?" he questioned.

"My calves and Achilles are sore. I think we should work on mobility, Jes," said Sanjay.

"Oh, you mean the thing I've been telling you to work on for the past four years?" I retorted.

Insert moment of calculated silence.

"Yes," he admitted.

As you can see, I was not the source of our second teachable moment. But I knew I had to capitalize on the opportunity. I wanted to remind Sanjay of the many, many, *many* times I told him to focus on mobility. I *really* wanted to rub that in. But I didn't.

As a trainer, you don't get these open doors that often. When you do, you've got to walk through them and start building new and consistent habits that will really pay off.

If Sanjay's story reminds you of yourself a little—great! That means you've opened the door to change. It means you know that striving to improve your health and fitness habits can pay off. These habits aren't just about playing more pickleball. They can also improve your overall well-being. Knowing that improved health habits will produce a significant return is the first step.

True change comes with the second step, and that's when things get challenging. The second step is taking action.

You'll make changes to your current lifestyle, learn new things, develop new habits, and push past your comfort zone.

Your beliefs about yourself, your potential, and what it really takes to succeed will be challenged. Sanjay went from a lofty goal he didn't feel passionate about to finding true joy in pursuing his well-being. Combine this joy with his passion for pickleball, and now he's motivated to be more fit, active, and mobile.

When you recognize the value of investing time into your health, start setting goals and make changes, you might feel more vulnerable than you care to admit. Don't let it stop you. That's when all the good stuff starts to happen!

I'm sure it wasn't always easy for Sanjay to let me boss him around and hear my sarcastic quips in response to some of his goals. I'm sure he felt vulnerable sometimes, but he also knew that I had his best interests at heart. I think (and hope) he realized that the results of being pushed outside his comfort zone outweighed the discomfort of the process.

Take-Home Points

1. Set a goal that inspires you to find joy in realizing the best version of yourself in health and fitness. Don't try to emulate someone else.

2. Consistency in healthy habits is key to creating real change.

3. Taking action to reach your goal will push you out of your comfort zone. Don't give up when things are tough. Stick to your plan, and you'll see results.

4

Wellness Habits for Longevity

Now you know who you're dealing with as your trainer, you're feeling motivated, and you've got some perspective on goal setting. So let's talk about some of the mental skills you'll need to master in order to make exercise, nutrition, and wellness part of your lifestyle.

No matter how fit or healthy you are now, being your best starts with having the right mentality for success. I like to break it down into three basics: what I call the ABCs of a winning mindset.

Awareness

Believe it or not, becoming your best requires more than learning what to do for exercise, nutrition, and wellness. If you want lasting change, you have to know how to do it and keep doing it—even if the going gets tough. And by "tough," I mean when life gets stressful, there are too many demands on your time, or you've lost your motivation, to name a few examples.

Developing a higher awareness of self will help you recognize how you respond to and manage stress. This is one of the most significant factors in achieving your health and fitness goals. This awareness will also help you figure out what motivates or deters you from taking action. You can then realistically evaluate what is possible for you to achieve with the time, tools, and genetics you have.

Balance

Your success will increase exponentially when you recognize and plan for the fact that your goals are not on an island. They will be influenced by the other priorities and challenges in your life.

Wellness goals should focus on forming habits and finding ways to adapt and balance the rest of your life demands. These goals will help you progress steadily forward. Otherwise, you risk forcing yourself down a path for a few weeks, hitting a roadblock, feeling defeated, and starting the cycle all over again. The same is true with finding a balance between exercise and nutrition and learning how to balance your nutrition throughout the day.

Consistency

Practicing the same result-producing habits consistently is the greatest indicator of your success. Being able to stick to any result-producing plan, even when you are only partially successful, is the name of the game!

I get frustrated by many of the programs on the market today because they promise amazing results in a short period of time. These promises often offer no context for how to fit these actions into your life, like the time required or the lifestyle or psychology necessary to achieve the results. They are nearly impossible to stick with long-term. These programs can be a beneficial tool in your fitness and nutrition toolbox. But the most important thing you can do for yourself is to create a plan that works year in and year out.

Instead of trying to force yourself to take action and feeling guilty if you fail, try shifting your mindset. Look toward starting the process by understanding and mastering the ABCs surrounding your goal. Then watch as your actions and habits fall into place.

It's Never Too Late to Get Started

Starting healthy habits when you're young can pay off in spades. But don't give up hope if you've been neglecting yourself for the past few decades. In my years as a trainer, I've helped clients of all ages—including people in their 80s—start exercising consistently. And they are absolutely amazed at what they are capable of doing.

As you read through this section, take it to heart that these wellness habits can be transformational when you practice them consistently. When I speak to people about wellness, fitness, or nutrition, I often hear the phrase, "Oh, that's obvious." This response is often used to deflect from the fact that the person is not taking action to implement important and life-changing habits.

Do your best to let these wellness habits percolate into your daily routine. Watch as you start to feel better and see yourself playing better and more frequently because of your new and improved choices.

Practice These Wellness Habits

Here are some great tips that will help you create a foundation of health and wellness you can build on:

- Eat whole and plant-based foods.
- Make sure your meat, poultry, and fish are prepared in their healthiest forms.
- Avoid sugar and processed foods.
- Limit your alcohol intake to one or fewer drinks per day.
- Avoid illegal drugs and misusing prescription drugs.
- Get at least 30 minutes of physical activity that safely elevates your heart rate most days of the week.
- Sleep 7–8½ hours a night.
- Wear sunscreen and sunglasses.
- Reach and maintain a healthy weight.
- Don't start smoking, or get help to quit.
- Wear a helmet when riding a bike and wear protective gear for sports.

- Wear your seat belt.
- Don't text and drive.
- Regularly visit the doctor and the dentist. Keep a list of questions and concerns you want to discuss in your phone's "notes" app. This allows you to add to the list as things occur to you.

Know Your Risk Factors

If you're anything like me, you prefer to assume that your health is fine and that risk factors don't apply to you. I think that is what most strong-willed individuals prefer to believe. We want to feel strong and in control of our own health. And that's why I have to remind myself that sometimes the best thing to do is listen to the experts.

Understanding risk factors allows you to take your health into your own hands and improve your chances for good long-term health.[1] When I refer to risk factors, I mean your genetics, age, sex, family health history, lifestyle, and more. Some risk factors, you must live with; for example, heart disease may run in your family. But others are within your control, like your lifestyle, diet, and physical activity level.

Having a risk factor does not mean something bad will definitely happen. It simply means you should acknowledge the possibility of something harming or negatively affecting your health. Awareness of risk factors gives you the opportunity to take preventive measures, which could potentially save your life. Keep records of your family and personal health history to use as a guide for making smart health decisions.

Here's an example. Let's say high blood pressure runs in your family, and you've been unable to control your blood pressure with diet and exercise. In this case, your doctor might recommend blood pressure medication. Knowing your family's health history as it relates to blood pressure should be part of your decision when it comes to medication.[1]

Track These Key Health Indicators

Key health indicators are tests that help you maintain good health and longevity. Usually, your family physician monitors these tests. Knowing your health indicator numbers and watching their change or consistency over time is a great long-term habit.

By tracking these indicators, you can recognize when you need to address any concerning changes. If your numbers remain at a consistent, healthy rate, you can rest assured that your health is in great standing. These numbers can also help motivate you to positively influence your health outcomes with new habits.

There is no hard-and-fast list of key health indicators, but you can start with these:

- blood pressure
- resting heart rate
- cholesterol

- triglycerides
- fasting blood sugar
- BMI or body fat percentage
- bone density[2]

Practicing your wellness tips and tracking your key health indicators will lead you to better health and fitness. It will also help you have a gauge of your health over time. Knowing your numbers can empower you to make great health choices. That being said, even if you don't have data-driven feedback, if you feel something is "off" when it comes to your health, see a doctor. You'll want to make sure nothing more serious is going on.

Since pickleball is a sport that we're hoping to help you play for life, playing with the understanding that your health changes over time is key. For women, this might mean paying more attention to bone density changes to prevent orthopedic problems. For men, it might be as simple as making sure that unrepaired hernia from 10 years ago finally gets attention.

In my years as a trainer, I've had many clients over 65 with osteopenia and unrepaired hernias go years without giving it a second thought. The difference is, when you take up a new sport and plan to play until you're 100, these things shift from "nothing to worry about" to risk factors for injury. Take care of yourself, and keep an eye on areas of previous injury so you can play for life!

Take-Home Points

1. Achieving your goals requires not only physical performance but mental performance as well. Be **aware** of yourself, **balanced** in your life demands, and **consistent** in following your plan.

2. Picking up new healthy habits at any age will benefit you—it's never too late!

3. Overwhelmed by the number of healthy habits you "should" be doing? Pick one each day and focus on that. Small steps forward are still steps forward.

5

Crafting Your Own Fitness & Nutrition Plan

If you've been playing pickleball for any length of time, you've probably observed the wide range of pickleballers. Players range from school kids to retirees over the age of 70 and everything in between.

You could be in great shape and doing all the right things. Or, you might feel a little lost and be wondering how to even get started. No matter where you fall on the spectrum, every passionate pickleballer wonders, "Is there anything more I can do to play a better game of pickleball?"

The answer is *yes*—by getting in better shape, eating healthier, and following the principles I've outlined in my Lean Code pillars. No matter what your starting point, in this chapter I hope to help you feel like you can take yourself to the next level.

The Three Pillars

Generally speaking, most people feel they "know what to do" when it comes to getting in shape and eating right. Wouldn't you agree? Then why do so many miss the mark? Why does that outcome they so desperately want stay just out of reach?

A few common reasons are lack of motivation, inconsistency, injury, not knowing how to manage an injury, or fear of injury. There can also be psychological reasons, such as a lack of accurate knowledge about getting in shape. Other people don't have objective measures for the process. And still others lack self-awareness or are unable to tolerate the discomfort.

Whenever I work with clients or have a casual conversation with someone about fitness goals, I'm always looking for that unseen roadblock. If I can help them with that, my work is done!

Over the years, I've developed a three-step process that I call "The Lean Code." I use this format to reveal roadblocks and share my knowledge of the three important components of achieving fitness and performance goals. Each element of the Lean Code is broken down into smaller pieces that you can work on one step at a time.

As you start to incorporate the bite-sized pieces into your daily life, you can create a structured system. Your system should work with *your* goals, the time *you* have available, and where *you* are in your life right now.

The Lean Code Pillar #1: Eat Lean

Eating lean is not a restrictive diet. In fact, when it comes to eating lean, you make the rules. Use the principles as your guide, but structure it to fit your lifestyle, your traditions, and your palate.

How do you get there?

- add superfoods
- reduce sugar
- control portions
- stay hydrated
- include plenty of fiber
- add protein and healthy fats

Following these principles will give you micro- and macro-nutrient balance. This balance will help you reduce cravings, maintain a healthy weight, and perform at your best. Instead of extreme restriction, focus on eating in balance and with purpose, and do it 85 percent of the time.

When it comes to nutrition, don't try to do it all at once. Tackle one element of eating lean at a time. Use the mentality of success, the ABCs (awareness, balance, and consistency), to set action-based goals that help you create new habits around each "eat lean" principle.

The Lean Code Pillar #2: Train Lean

Use science-based methods to create an exercise plan that maximizes caloric output and improves performance while reducing risk of injury. Combine that with time efficiency and making fitness as convenient and structured as possible.

How do you get there?

- assessment of injuries and tools available for training
- HIIT cardio
- mobility and flexibility
- posture, core, and form
- strength training

Your training plan should complement your pickleball goals. If you get plenty of cardiovascular activity from playing, shift your focus to strength training, core, mobility, and flexibility. If you play twice per week, try strength training two to three times per week on the off days. Practice your mobility work before you play and passive stretching after you play. An efficient, well-balanced training schedule will improve your performance on the court and help prevent common injuries.

The Lean Code Pillar #3: Live Lean

The Lean Code is not just about eating twigs and berries while busting your butt 24/7/365. Living lean means being strategic and setting up result-producing habits that include:

- *Stress reduction:* Stress is a major cause of binge eating, excessive drinking, and lack of energy for exercise.
- *Physical restoration:* Lack of recovery and limitations in mobility or flexibility are huge causes of injury and reinjury.

- *Preparation:* Get ready for the next event, whether it's a race, workout, or game.

How do you get there?

- stress management
- time management
- mental fitness strategies
- mind-body strategies
- restoration and recovery
- learning to pivot

Planning ahead, reducing stress, and giving yourself proper recovery time will keep you on target and prevent self-sabotage. You can work alone, with a friend, a motivating community, a knowledgeable coach, or any combination of the above. Utilizing each of these options increases your chances of success by holding you accountable and keeping you on track.

Once you have the right information and tools, you have the power to change your life. Create a system that works for you every day to have a lean lifestyle. Combine that with support from your community, and the sky's the limit!

Take-Home Points

1. Identify what roadblocks you face, and learn to eat lean, train lean, and live lean in a way that fits your lifestyle.

2. A community of folks with similar goals of improving fitness may help keep you on track. Share your goals with family or friends—they just might want to join you on this journey.

6

Nutrition 101

I started experimenting with diets when I was a child. I can vividly remember trying the "noodles and water diet" at age 10. At that point in my young life, the word *diet* had no positive or negative emotions attached to it. It was just something the adults were doing, so I felt I should do it too.

Growing up, I learned from society, adults, and kids at school that girls were supposed to want to lose weight. I learned that we should also be critical of ourselves and how we looked. I was an athlete and got decent grades, so I absorbed positive messages too. But both the positive and negative messages were strong.

Over time, these strong opposing messages created somewhat of a battlefield within my psyche. By my late teens, "the me who accepted me" battled "the me they said I should be." My decisions about food and dieting were the result of both sides. One minute I was doing one thing, two weeks later another thing. A month went by, and I was back to the beginning. I had no clue!

My young self was just trying to figure it out and wanted to feel good. As a result, I fought and lost (thankfully!) many diet battles, including:

- the noodles and water diet (lasted five hours),
- the eat nothing diet (lasted six hours),
- the cabbage soup diet (lasted three days), and
- the broth and vegetables diet (lasted two days).

I never considered how these diets might impact my performance or long-term health. I just figured I would lose weight doing them—and that's all I really cared about (I'm not sure why, since I wasn't overweight).

I started to learn snippets of information about nutrition. I decided that eating healthy would improve my appearance and my performance. So I started eating "fat-free." I thought I had made a really wise and healthy choice. I was certain I had put the unhealthy myths behind me. As I write this, I'm still amazed I was thinking this way at 17, but I was. I thought I was eating the right foods to help me be healthy and look good.

Time went on, and I realized that instead of eating normal foods, I was eating mostly fat-free foods that replaced fat with sugar. I had no energy, which prompted me to eat more fat-free, high-sugar foods . . . and I did not lose weight. Instead, I gained! For years and years, I had constant sugar cravings. I ate more sour gummy bears than you could ever imagine. I also became awesome at making baked goods—especially late at night.

Whether I dieted or not didn't matter—the cravings never went away. I knew I had to fix this issue, but I wasn't sure how. Eventually, I realized sugar was not good for me, so I tried the Atkins diet . . . the opposite extreme! Another frustrating result ensued. The only thing the Atkins diet did for me was help me gain 15 pounds. I felt terrible about my ability to be healthy and control my weight and appearance.

Luckily, I was studying kinesiology at the time and my mentor was extremely interested in nutrition. He even wrote a guidebook for his clients and those like me, his mentee. It took me years to learn and apply the things his guidebook recommended. But I knew I had finally found something that actually worked to improve my health, performance, and physique!

Today, I enjoy food and I have control over my cravings. I eat fresh and healthy most of the time, and sometimes I indulge without feeling guilty. I maintain a very lean and healthy physique, and I have tons of energy.

Since I'm a trainer, many people approach me with nutrition and fitness questions. When we're talking about training, people are usually totally engaged and keep picking my brain for more info. On the contrary, conversations about food last around 10 seconds max . . . People may provide vague answers or may avoid the subject entirely.

Nutrition and dieting come with a lot of baggage. Everything—from our packed daily schedules to personal beliefs, self-esteem, and family traditions—influences our choices. Combine those things with the ever-evolving body of nutrition research and the powerful influence of the food and supplement industries; now we've got a huge number of potential approaches to nutrition.

I've found that conversations about nutrition and diet bring up a wide variety of internal barriers. I've heard many approaches to "healthy eating." Some of them are quite entertaining:

- "I know exactly how to eat. Whenever I want to lose weight, I only allow myself to eat food I don't like."
- "I don't think the specifics of nutrition matter that much, as long as you don't overeat."
- "I think everyone on the planet should be a vegan."
- "Fast food once a week is fine."
- "Intermittent fasting cures disease."

The variety of beliefs is never-ending. Some people find nutrition to be simple, while for others it is a continual struggle. One of the biggest reasons people struggle to shift their nutrition is that doing so is too far outside their comfort zones. It goes against the grain of family routines and work demands. Or it doesn't fit with their schedules and feels too overwhelming and restrictive.

No matter what their rationale, somewhere deep down they know that improving their nutrition will improve their health, their energy levels, and therefore, their pickleball game. Nutrition also directly impacts the key health indicators we covered in the wellness section. When you improve your key health indicators, you can play pickleball for years to come—hopefully for life.

So let's dive a little deeper into nutrition. Let me start by asking you, have you ever stopped yourself midbite and asked, "Why am I eating this?" If you really want to make a change in your nutrition, it's one of the most powerful questions you can ask—especially if all you hear is crickets as an answer. Before you start your next diet, remember that a clear goal and plan based on your genetics, lifestyle, and activity level are key.

Nutrition for Health & Weight Loss

I recommend focusing on "I'm eating for my health" as a goal if you want to:

- lose 12 pounds or more,
- reduce chronic inflammation,
- improve blood sugar regulation,
- achieve healthier cholesterol and triglyceride levels, and
- address gastrointestinal (GI) issues, allergies, or other health issues.

Your action steps should include:

- eliminating problem-provoking foods,
- improving the quality of the foods you eat,
- controlling your portions, and
- introducing consistency.

Nutrition for a Better Physique

I recommend focusing on "I'm eating for my physique" as a goal if you want to:

- lose fewer than 12 pounds,
- increase lean muscle, and
- reduce body fat.

Your action steps should include:

- balancing macros,
- food tracking, and
- nutrient timing.

Nutrition for Performance

I recommend "I eat to perform" as a goal if you:

- want to improve your fitness or sport performance,
- don't want to lose any weight, and
- don't wish to improve your physique.

Take the same actions as the physique steps just mentioned and adjust your nutrition based on your training load and recovery needs. Determine nutrient deficiencies that you may need to address with supplements. Learning how to integrate nourishing foods in the right amounts will:

- transform your energy levels,
- improve your overall health, and
- give you the fuel you need for a great workout.

If you get off track with your eating, having an "eat lean" plan will help you refocus and reset. This plan gives you a simple way to guide yourself back to a good macronutrient balance, proper portions, and healthy foods that are free of preservatives and other additives. Here are some of the elements of nutrition you need to understand and apply if you want awesome results.

Eat Lean Basics

Below are some general guidelines to help you get back on track, improve your health, and reach an ideal weight. These basic principles can be adjusted to fit your dietary needs and supply the nutrients you need.

1. Eat superfoods as often as possible, which include:
   a. whole, unprocessed foods with few ingredients, like fresh fruits and vegetables;
   b. grass-fed meat and poultry;
   c. fish that is sustainably wild caught or raised on eco-friendly farms;
   d. organic and non-genetically modified organism (GMO) foods; and
   e. nutrient-dense foods (meaning they have a high concentration of vitamins and minerals per calorie).

2. Limit added sugars[1]
   a. *Women:* Maximum 25 grams per day
   b. *Men:* Maximum 35 grams per day

3. Stay hydrated[2]
   a. *Women:* 2–3 liters of water per day
   b. *Men:* 3–4 liters of water per day
   c. Drink more if you are exercising intensely

4. Consume sufficient daily fiber[3]
   a. *Women:* 25–35 grams per day
   b. *Men:* 35–45 grams per day

5. Know your portion sizes
   a. Serving size of protein should be about the size of your palm
   b. Serving size of fats should be the size of your thumb
   c. Serving size of carbs from veggies should be about the size of your hand

6. Get adequate protein
   a. 30 percent of your total daily calories should consist of healthy protein

7. Include healthy fats
   a. *Animal fats:* Grass-fed, organic, sustainably raised meat; organic poultry; pasture-raised eggs
   b. *Fish and seafood:* Wild, sustainably caught or eco-friendly, farmed fatty fish—sardines, mackerel, herring, cod, salmon, and shellfish

   c. *Dairy and dairy substitutes:* Grass-fed butter, ghee, unsweetened nut and seed milks (almond, cashew, hemp, hazelnut)
   d. *Nuts and seeds:* Almonds, macadamia nuts, walnuts, pecans, and brazil nuts; hemp, chia, pumpkin, sesame, and flax seeds
   e. *Oils:* Organic, virgin, cold-pressed coconut oil and olive oil; medium-chain triglycerides (MCT) oil, organic expeller pressed flax seed oil, avocado oil, and hemp oil
   f. *Whole food fats:* Avocado, olives, cacao butter, and so on.

It probably seems like a lot, doesn't it?

Honestly, there are a lot of things you can learn about nutrition—even more than what's listed here. But if you do not know how to apply the information in a practical manner . . . it's kind of pointless. Your nutrition choices impact your health on so many levels. It's worth it to put the effort in to get healthier. Trust me on this!

Take-Home Points

1. Ask yourself often, "Why am I eating this?" and proceed accordingly. Eating mindfully is the best way to stick with your goals.

2. Eat whole, unprocessed foods, increasing your intake of healthy nutrients.

3. Remember, what you put into your body directly impacts how it performs. Eat for your health.

PART 2
Train to Be a Better Player

Story from the Court

I've been playing sports since age four, when I could barely make contact with the T-ball. Even then, I loved sports because I could get outdoors and socialize with friends. I also loved being part of a team, learning and improving new skills, the thrill of winning, and ultimately, just having a lot of fun.

While I enjoyed sports of all kinds, field hockey captured my interest the most. It required complex strategy, exceptional fitness, teamwork, and creativity. Fast forward to college. I played Division 1 field hockey at the University of Michigan and served as team captain my senior year.

After graduation and the end of my field hockey career, I wanted to find something that would capture all the reasons why I started playing sports in the first place. For me, that was pickleball. I've been playing for almost five years, and I jump at any opportunity to get in the game!

Since I competed as a Division 1 athlete, I understand the value and necessity of training—both from a performance and injury prevention standpoint. Training allows for continuous growth in the sport and ensures your mind and body are ready for competition.

Now, in my role as a nurse, I clearly see the connection between training (or lack thereof) and sports injuries. You can often prevent back strains, ankle injuries, shoulder pain, knee pain, and more with regular dynamic stretching, physical activity, and training. As a nurse, I strive to help my patients age in a healthy way. That's why I am constantly educating people on the need for regular physical activity.

Fortunately, pickleball can serve just that need! Pickleball allows for different levels of exertion and mobility, depending on how you play the game. And whether you're a Division 1 athlete or have never played sports in your life, pickleball is movement, it's socializing, and it's fun. See you on the courts!

—*Eliza Stein, RN, Chicago, IL*

Part 2: Train to Be a Better Player

By now, you know that pickleball is a sport that appeals to the elite, the elderly, and everyone else. This wide variety of participants means that *you* might land anywhere, from beginner athlete to super fit. Regardless of your athletic ability, pickleball rating, age, or previous injuries, you can train to be a better player.

Ask yourself where you are right now and what you want to achieve without being too limiting or pessimistic. I've trained many a client who, after giving themselves over to the process and staying committed, were truly amazed at what they were capable of. They also discovered how good they could feel. The potential of an individual is often beyond their perception.

Stay open-minded to what your potential might be with the right tools and guidance. Let yourself dream a little and see what comes to the surface. Bring those goals to the table and combine them with realistic measures. Consider your availability, tools, resources, and knowledge. Then set goals that are specific to you. Write down your goals, knowing that you've faced different challenges and have different gifts and life experiences than others. Our unique life experiences are our "playing fields," in a sense. And we must teach ourselves to dominate them, whatever they may be.

In this section, we have outlined the foundation for you to train to be a better pickleball player. In many ways, this section is just the tip of the iceberg. At the same time, it gives even the elite player a road map to improvement. Please try to keep your personal goals in mind as you continue reading.

7

Core & Posture

Does your lower back ache when you wake up in the morning? How about your neck and upper back after a long day of work at the computer? Do your shoulders feel tight, but you don't know why?

Many of my clients attribute these chronic aches and pains to "getting older" (even when they are under 40!). But it often has to do with chronically poor posture combined with weak core muscles. Many of these aches and pains can be eliminated or greatly reduced with improved posture, stretching, mobility, and core strengthening.

Posture is one of the first things I talk about with my new clients. I give them a general understanding of how to sit, stand, and train without slouching, overusing their necks, or putting undue stress on their lower backs. Practicing neutral posture helps them focus on improving their quality of movement inside and outside of the gym. When you train and move well, you reduce your risk of injury and improve your athletic performance.

Having neutral posture doesn't mean you need to have perfect posture at every moment—you don't. But if you want to improve your level of play, practicing perfect posture will help you gain awareness of your body position during various activities.

Through improved body awareness, you learn to move more safely and efficiently. Training improves your mobility around your joints and strengthens all the sides of your joints. It also corrects any imbalances that may have developed over time, so each joint is in its safest position at rest and in motion.

The terms *neutral posture* and *neutral spine* mean that each joint is in an ideal resting position. This is the position that produces the least tension or pressure on nerves, tendons, muscles, and bones. It also positions your muscles at their resting length—neither contracted nor stretched. Muscles at this length can develop maximum force most efficiently.

Maintaining your neutral posture is as simple as stacking. Stack your shoulders over your hips and your hips over the center of your feet. Do this while maintaining the natural curve of your spine, a tight stomach, a neutral pelvis, and soft knees.

Although having neutral posture is the healthiest position, people tend to round out their upper back or rotate their pelvis back and let their stomach flop. This often happens if you have a sit-down job, drive frequently, or even when you get fatigued during exercise.

Standing or sitting in one of these positions might feel natural, but "nonneutral" positions can be detrimental to your body and put you at risk for injury. Standing, sitting, and exercising with neutral posture means your body is more likely to be in a good position during play. You'll also

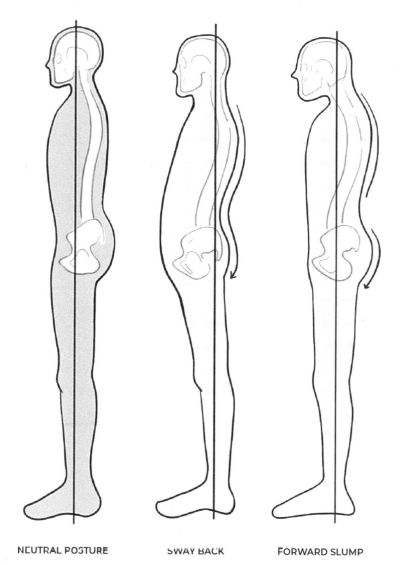

NEUTRAL POSTURE   SWAY BACK   FORWARD SLUMP

look taller and more confident and reduce aches, pains, and your risk of injury!

Perfect Neutral Posture

- Ears, shoulders, hips, knees, and ankles are "stacked" in alignment from the side view.
- Shoulders are down and back, under the ears, or just in front of them.
- Shoulders are the same height (one is not higher than the other).
- Hips are the same height (unless one leg is longer than the other).
- Weight is evenly distributed between both legs.
- Weight is over the midfoot or in the heels, depending on what you are doing.
- Stomach is slightly tightened, as if someone had just walked by and surprised you with a tap in the stomach.

Postural Deviations

The "forward slump" and "swayback" postures are two common postural deviations. These are postures we want to avoid when we're striving for neutral posture.

Forward Slump

The forward slump is when you slump your upper back and head forward while maintaining the natural position of your lower back. I also call this the C posture.

The forward slump may result from many hours of computer work, driving, and looking down at your cell phone. Over time, the muscles in the chest, shoulders, and neck tighten and those in the upper back become relatively weak. This posture can cause neck and shoulder pain and can eventually lead to injury.

Swayback

The swayback is when you hold your shoulders and upper back in the neutral position, but your lower back has an exaggerated lumbar curve. You may notice that when you stand or walk, it looks like you are leaning slightly back. The exaggerated lumbar curve is the result of weakness in the glutes and core muscles combined with tightness in the hamstrings, hip flexors, and lower back muscles.

There are many variations of these two common postural deviations, and you may fit somewhere in between. If you have less-than-ideal posture, focusing on proper posture can protect your joints from injury and reduce pain.

Evaluation

To get an objective record of your posture progress, have someone take three pictures of you from the front and side:

1. standing naturally,
2. ready to address the ball, and
3. in the ready position during play.

Look at the photos. Do you see any postural deviations? What do you notice? Check for:

- a forward slump,
- a swayback,
- a floppy stomach, and
- locked knees.

Exercises

The following exercises can help you improve your posture. By studying your own posture, you can identify which exercises apply specifically to you. Then you can incorporate some or all of them into your daily exercise routine. Descriptions and photos of each exercise are also included here. For a video guide and further info, visit https://pickleballbody.com/videos.

Posture Exercises

- Snow Angel on Foam Roller
- Scapula Protraction/Retraction
- Double Chin
- Chest Clasp Stretch
- Kneeling Reach-Over Stretch
- Cat/Cow/Table

Snow Angel on Foam Roller
(see Appendix for further details on foam rolling)

- Using a foam roller, lie down lengthwise directly on the roller with your bottom at one end, head at the other, and spine directly over the roller.

- Place your arms out to your sides, making a *T* with your palms up.

- Keeping your arms fairly straight, slowly arch your arms over your head, stopping at brief intervals to feel the stretch.

Scapula Protraction/Retraction

- Stand in neutral posture and draw in your navel to engage your core.

- Place your arms out to your sides, making a *T*. Bend your elbows 90 degrees so that your fingers are pointing up and your palms are facing forward.

- Keeping your elbows straight and your back neutral, squeeze your shoulder blades together. Make sure you have a large space between your ears and shoulders while squeezing. Hold for 3 seconds.

- While maintaining your elbows straight out, ear-to-shoulder space, and neutral spine, release the squeeze in your shoulder blades.

- Repeat 15 times at moderate speed, being careful not to engage your neck and trapezius (muscles at the back of the neck and shoulders).

Double Chin

- Stand or kneel with neutral spine and your core engaged. Let your arms rest at your sides.

- Keep your shoulders down and back.

- With your mouth closed and your eyes even with the horizon (not tilting your head), gently draw your chin toward the back of the room so that it feels like you are making a double chin. You should feel gentle activation of the muscles in the back of your head at the base of your skull.

- Hold for 5 seconds and return to the start position. Repeat 5 times.

Chest Clasp Stretch

- Stand tall with neutral posture and knees soft.

- Reach behind your back and lace your fingers together.

- Using your laced fingers as leverage, pull your shoulder blades together and open your chest. You should feel like your collar bones are as far apart as possible and your chest and shoulders are being stretched.

- Lift your hands up and away from your bottom if you can, but this is not required. Use the intensity of your stretch as a guide.

Kneeling Reach-Over Stretch

- Starting on your hands and knees, move your bottom toward your heels while keeping your arms straight.
- With your arms straight out in front of you, you should start to feel a stretch along the sides of your back.
- Move both hands slightly to your right, across the midline of your body. Side bend ever so slightly to feel a stretch on the opposite side.
- Repeat, reaching the other direction.

Cat/Cow/Table

- *Start from table pose:* Get on your hands and knees, making sure your hands are directly below your shoulders and your knees are directly below your hips. Draw your navel in to engage your core.
- *Cat pose:* With your core strongly engaged, slowly tuck your tailbone and round your shoulders, allowing your head to drop down. Slowly transition to cow pose.
- *Cow pose:* Push your shoulders down, lift your chin, and arch your back while keeping your core engaged to at least 50 percent.
- Repeat this sequence 5 times with control and core engagement.

Core Strength

As Sanjay and I are self-proclaimed health and fitness nerds, core strength and rotational movement are probably two of our favorite subjects. This is where the rubber meets the road!

Core strength and rotational movement are your building blocks for improved speed, a transfer of power from your lower to upper body, and rotational movement. Rotational movement is central to any racquet sport—including pickleball, of course!

Throughout my years as a trainer, I've had many conversations that include the words *core*, *core strength*, *core stability*, and *core training*. Clients, friends, athletes, people interested in weight loss, yogis . . . *everybody* talks about core.

Some people have a different definition of *core* than I do. Athletes and coaches tend to look at core exercises as a method of improving athletic performance. General fitness enthusiasts often refer to the core as the "midsection." Bodybuilding-oriented people tend to think of the core as a means to develop six-pack abs, like Sanjay has. ☺

While these definitions are all somewhat correct, none of them is specific. The definition of *core* varies based on who you are talking to, their fitness goals, and their exercise background. The nonspecific nature of these overlapping definitions can cause confusion for someone who wants to incorporate core strength training into their fitness regimen.

It's not wrong to say the core is the midsection, because the core is in the middle of the body. And the core does include the rectus abdominis (a.k.a., the six-pack ab area), so "working the abs" is certainly part of core strength training. But your core is about more than a flat stomach or muscular abs.

Since we are learning about core strength to improve your pickleball game, let's look at the core from an athletic perspective. We'll dive further into what core strength training means to an athlete and how it can improve performance. You'll learn why the core is important to improving your game and how to strengthen and activate it during play.

For us fitness nerds, the core is the lumbopelvic hip complex (LPHC) and refers to the lumbar spine, pelvis, and hip musculoskeletal structures. These muscles protect and stabilize the spine and pelvis. In the fitness world, there a variety of opinions on exactly which muscles are included.

This is a general illustration of the muscles that most fitness professionals consider to be part of the core as it relates to the athlete.

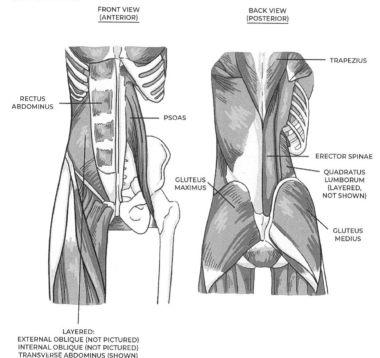

FRONT VIEW
(ANTERIOR)

BACK VIEW
(POSTERIOR)

TRAPEZIUS

RECTUS
ABDOMINUS

PSOAS

ERECTOR SPINAE

QUADRATUS
LUMBORUM
(LAYERED,
NOT SHOWN)

GLUTEUS
MAXIMUS

GLUTEUS
MEDIUS

LAYERED:
EXTERNAL OBLIQUE (NOT PICTURED)
INTERNAL OBLIQUE (NOT PICTURED)
TRANSVERSE ABDOMINUS (SHOWN)

The above photo illustrates just how many muscles work together to form the core. And as mentioned, this is meant to give you a general understanding.

You see, the "core" muscles are not just the muscles you can see and feel on the surface of the body. Some of the most important core muscles are layered underneath the superficial muscles. Because of this, it might be a challenge for you to know and learn how to use them. Don't worry, I will help you! Learning where these muscles are and how to use them is an important step in understanding how to activate your core during athletic movement. Here's a simple way to define the core: everything below the rib cage and above the hips.

What Does the Core Actually Do?

The muscles termed the *core* work together to:

- protect your lower back (when used properly),
- stabilize, support, and protect your spine and pelvis,
- improve your balance and stability,
- facilitate rotational movement, and
- transfer power between your upper and lower body.

The Kinetic Chain

Thomas Reid once said, "A chain is only as strong as its weakest link."[1] Imagine your body as a chain, with each limb being a separate link. Your feet, lower legs, upper legs, core, and shoulders are links in that chain. This will give you a great metaphoric understanding of the kinetic chain and the importance of core strength.

Every part of your body is connected to—and therefore impacted by—other parts of your body. The kinetic chain describes how the body transfers force from the ground, through your body, and into your paddle. The core is a key link in your kinetic chain. The stronger and more active your core, the more effectively you will transfer energy and power from your legs into your upper body and your shots.

When an athlete initiates movement, their legs drive powerfully into the ground. Then the ground "pushes" the same amount of force back into the body. This is called the ground reaction force. Your *stable* and *balanced* contact with the ground is the first link in your kinetic chain. This contact allows force to travel from the ground, through your legs, into your core, through your upper body, and into your paddle.

Your core is the primary mechanism for the transfer of power between your upper and lower body. If your core is weak, or as I like to say, "lazily flopping around," the force from your lower body will dissipate. It won't maintain its power as it moves to your upper body and paddle.

This is one of the main reasons core strength is so important in athletics, including racquet and paddle sports like pickleball. Having a strong core also really helps with your dinking game. Effective dinking—just getting the ball over the net and keeping it in the kitchen—requires squatting and using many of your core muscles. After playing a few hours with players who have really good soft games, your glutes and quads may be really sore. You've essentially been doing a ton of squats!

Exercises

The exercises listed here will help you create a solid foundation to improve core strength. As you learn which exercises apply specifically to you, incorporate them into your daily exercise routine. Descriptions and photos of each exercise are also included here. For a video guide and further info, visit https://pickleballbody.com/videos.

Core Exercises

- Straight Arm and Forearm Plank
- Side Plank
- Lower Body Hold
- Antirotation

Straight Arm and Forearm Plank

 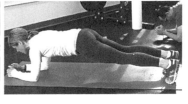

- The plank trains your muscles to hold neutral spine against outside forces—in this case, gravity. As you get stronger, your muscles will be more capable of protecting your spine during sports and other activities.

- Start from table pose, with your arms directly below your shoulders and your navel drawn in to activate your core.

- Straighten both knees and place both feet on the ground about hip width apart.

- Hold yourself in neutral spine and avoid rounding your upper back, arching your lower back, or holding your hips too high (out of neutral). Think ear, shoulder, hip, knee, and ankle in one straight line, like a plank of wood.

- If you start to feel any discomfort in your lower back, put one knee down but continue to hold neutral spine and activate your core. Even with this modification, the exercise can still be very challenging.

- If you still feel back pain, put both knees down and continue to keep your spine neutral and your core active.

- Try this method from both the straight arm (high plank) and forearm (low plank) position.

Side Plank

- Lie down on your left side with your left forearm on the ground lifting your upper body. Make sure your left elbow is stacked directly under the left shoulder.

- Start with your legs stacked on top of one another and your knees bent at 90 degrees. If this leg position feels easy, gradually progress yourself to straight legs.

- Engaging your core, lift your left hip off the ground, making a straight line from your knees to left elbow. Raise your right hand into the air, making a *T* shape with your arms.

- If you are new to this exercise, start with a 30 second hold. Rest 5 seconds and repeat on the opposite side.

- If you are unable to keep your core engaged or hold a neutral posture, return to having your knees bent at 90 degrees.

Lower Body Hold

The **lower body hold** helps you connect with and recruit the muscles in your lower core and pelvic floor. Even though this exercise seems simple, it can dramatically improve your overall core strength. Many of us have a limited ability to intentionally recruit these muscles. The more you practice isometric holds like this one, the better you will be able to access these muscles during activities like pickleball!

- Lie down on your back with your knees bent and feet flat on the floor. Make sure your lower back and pelvis are in a neutral position. Too much of an arch in your lower back or your hips being tilted slightly forward mean you need to tuck your tail under to find neutral.

- Draw your navel in toward your spine to activate your core muscles.

- Lift one leg off the floor, keeping your knee bent at 90 degrees.

- If you can maintain your neutral lower back with one leg off the ground, lift the second leg off the ground. This is what I call the "base" position for the exercise.

- Make sure your core is active and your lower back is neutral. If they are, slowly straighten your knees until you feel the lower part of your core being challenged. Don't allow your back to move.

- Hold your legs at an angle that challenges your core for 60 seconds. Every 10 seconds, try to recruit 10 percent more of your core muscles. Pretend you're at a flexing contest at the beach, and whoever works the hardest wins!

- Some people will find this exercise quite challenging. Others will be tempted to straighten their legs and lower their feet to just above the ground. Rest assured, you do not need to lower your legs extremely close to the ground for this exercise to be effective. In fact, I recommend lowering them only as far as you need to feel your core engage. Then focus on recruiting 10 percent more every 10 seconds from a stationary position.

- Set a goal of 3 sets of 60-second holds. If you are new to this exercise, start with 15 seconds at a time, rest for 5, and repeat. You'll get stronger quickly when you practice consistently.

Antirotation

- This isometric core exercise requires a stretchable exercise band.

- Loop the band around a sturdy object, securing it to a fence, doorway, squat rack, or similar.

- Once the band is secured on one end, grab the other end with both hands and step to the side, lining up your shoulder with the anchor point on the band and standing far enough away that you feel significant tension in the band.

- Clasp your hands together along with the band. Lengthen your arms in front of you and form a triangle.

- Make sure your shoulders, chest, belly button, and hips are all facing the same direction, a 90-degree angle from the anchor point of the band.

- Use your core to hold yourself in neutral, and do not allow the tension of the band to rotate you toward the anchor point.

- Set the timer for 45 seconds and hold neutral posture. Do not let tension be lost in the band.

- The tension within the band will try to rotate your body. Engaging your core muscles will ensure you do not rotate, despite the band pulling you.

Take-Home Points

1. Practicing proper form and good posture protects your muscles from injury.

2. Core strength, flexibility, mobility, balance, and stability are the building blocks for rotational movement. Strong rotational movement is key to finding success in pickleball and avoiding injury.

3. Remember the kinetic chain: Every part of your body connects to your core. This is where you get your power from on the pickleball court.

8

Mobility & Flexibility

In my years as a trainer, my clients have given me quite a few nicknames and compared me to many evil characters. I've been called "Helga," "Nurse Ratched," "Border Patrol agent," "Vincent Price" (from Michael Jackson's "Thriller" video), and "the queen from *Alice in Wonderland*" (who shouts, "Off with their heads!").

You can probably guess that I'm a tough trainer, and my clients sometimes need an outlet. Not only do I have nicknames, but I hear plenty of sarcastic comments when I push my clients really hard. Comments often include "What?" "Are you kidding me?" "WTF," and "No way." Pretty funny, huh? I kept it clean, but there are many, many more.

It's all in good fun, really. I know that these comments are coping mechanisms people use to deal with having their limits pushed and to mitigate the anticipation of pain. The anticipation of pain, which happens in any tough workout, can elicit a low-level panic or a need to push back (hence the nicknames). Some people completely embrace it, others avoid it, and still others push against it. It just depends on your personal psychology.

One of the ways trainers can help people reduce fear of pain and injury is by teaching them to perform regular flexibility and mobility work. This doesn't necessarily reduce the name-calling or expletives. But it does build athletes' confidence that they are taking steps to prevent injury and improve the quality of their movement.

As I mentioned earlier, it was difficult for Sanjay to embrace the idea of regular stretching and mobility. Yes, he saw a few of his pickle pals get injured on the court, and that moved the needle significantly. But we still had a short journey to travel in what I like to call Sanjay's "days gone by" theory. Read on and I'll take you through it.

This, like so many other client stories, starts with the client refusing to admit they have a problem, ache, or pain. This stage can last anywhere from a few days to years. In Sanjay's case, one day he mentioned that he was having "a little bit" of foot pain. I've been training clients long enough to know what that means. It means he had been in pain for a while, and it was probably five times worse than he was admitting.

Clients don't tell me about pain because they really don't want it to take them away from what they are doing. In other words, "I'm not telling Jes this because it might mean I have to take a break from pickleball."

So when even the slightest mention of possible injury comes up, I ask a lot of questions. I try to find out what the real issue is and recommend steps to help. Remember, we are still on day one of this journey. There are many more to come.

I concluded that Sanjay was experiencing early stage plantar fasciitis. This condition can be very painful, and if you don't take action to mitigate it, it can require:

- a long period of rest (without pickleball),
- physical therapy,
- sleeping with foot braces,
- injections for pain, and
- surgery (in severe cases).

I told Sanjay all of this because I wanted him to take it seriously. I've seen many clients ignore plantar fasciitis for too long. Then they require serious adjustments and extensive treatment in order to heal. He listened and responded, "OK, got it. New motion-controlled shoes and do my stretches every day." But then came a dreaded long pause, followed by, ". . . but what about wearing better socks, Jes? Would that work?"

"What?" I articulated in my most reasonable voice, toning down my indignation. I realized Sanjay had no idea how serious this problem could get if he didn't take action.

"Well, back in high school basketball, I remember I had some foot pain, and as soon as I put on my tube sock, it went away. I mean, it totally took care of the problem!" said Sanjay.

You can envision the expression on my face, I'm sure.

"That was high school. Those are days gone by—you were 15 years old!" I replied. "I'm pretty sure a tube sock reminiscent of your high school basketball uniform will not cure plantar fasciitis."

A week later, we met for our weekly appointment. As we normally do, we went through our check-in process that includes a discussion about nutrition, exercise throughout the week, and any pain or injuries.

"The tube sock worked. It worked!" exclaimed Sanjay.

"What?! A tube sock? [Cue my silent death gaze directly at him.] What aren't you telling me?" I demanded.

"Well, I mean it worked while I played, but I still had pain after," mentioned Sanjay.

"Ah ha!" I had caught him.

"Well, it worked, and I think it will be fine. In fact, I have an idea for next week I'm going to try. I have a feeling this problem will be solved," he said.

"Fine, if you think this tube sock is going to be the solution, go ahead. Just promise me you will do your stretches and start looking for new motion-controlled shoes," I replied.

"OK," he conceded.

One week later. Same checklist.

"How is the foot pain, and how did your secret solution work?" I inquired.

"You know what my solution was? *Two* tube socks. Two tube socks and it worked. I swear it worked," Sanjay proclaimed. "Two tube socks, just like the old days. Problem solved."

I rolled my eyes. "OK."

Another week later. Same checklist. Although I wanted to, I did not sarcastically ask, "How did the two tube socks work?"

Sanjay admitted, "OK . . . so maybe the two-tube-sock theory wasn't the best. I still have pain. Veronica is threatening to make me stop playing because I'm limping around the house. What should I do?"

"I knew it!" I said. "I told you that those tube socks were not the answer!"

It was only after the tube sock theory was disproven that Sanjay fully embraced stretching and mobility work. Sanjay is not the only one who practices avoidance when it comes to pain. I can totally relate. I actually just pulled out an unopened bottle of ibuprofen from my gym bag and smiled because I can remember taking far more than the recommended amount before, during, and after volleyball tournaments. I was in my early 20s and took it to help with my knee and back pain. I had no clue how bad it was for my overall health.

I also didn't really understand that you could live pain free as an adult. I figured that was for the 20-year-olds and high schoolers. It took me more than a few years to stop using anti-inflammatories all together. It only happened because I've learned so much about injury prevention and postrehab training. Now I protect myself from new injuries and manage old ones with mobility work, foam rolling, core strength, and passive stretching.

It's hard convincing clients, and even trainers, to invest their time into doing these things as part of their training. But once they do, the difference is like night and day! Keep an open mind to mobility and stretching in your journey toward becoming a better player so that you can play for many years beyond your expectations.

Mobility & Flexibility: A Step *Everyone* Can Take to Improve Performance

"Notice that the stiffest tree is most easily cracked, while the bamboo or willow survive by bending with the wind."—Bruce Lee[1]

Occasionally, when I mention the term *mobility* in a conversation, someone asks me, "Well . . . what is mobility? Is it yoga or stretching or something?" I sometimes forget that *mobility* can be an obscure term outside of the fitness realm. Think of mobility as being able to:

- reach overhead to get something off the top shelf,
- bend down to pick up something off the floor, or
- reach into the back seat of your car to grab your purse without "tweaking" anything.

Mobility is also the ability to:

- get into a deep squat or perform Olympic lifts safely,
- have a running stride that improves your fastest 5k time, or
- play your best in pickleball numerous times a week and in tournaments on weekends.

Mobility is often confused with *flexibility* because these terms are intertwined. I like to tell my clients that flexibility is your passive range of motion, while mobility is your ability to take your joint through its range of motion while activating your surrounding muscles. More simply put, mobility is applied flexibility.

Having good flexibility and mobility reduces your risk of injury and improves the quality of your movement and athleticism. Let's learn more about the terms in this chapter.

Flexibility

flex·i·bil·i·ty [flek–*suh*–bil–i–tee], noun

1. Range of motion about a joint dependent on the condition of surrounding structures.[2]

The two most practiced forms of flexibility are as follows:

Dynamic stretching: You move through a challenging but comfortable range of motion repeatedly, usually 10 to 20 times. You can perform dynamic stretches **before a workout or game**. Ease into the range of motion as your blood flow increases and your joints, ligaments, tendons, and muscles warm up.

Static stretching: You hold a stretch in a challenging but comfortable position for 10 to 30 seconds. Usually, you should perform static stretches **after you work out or play a game**.

Most people know some basic stretches but struggle to do it on a regular basis. The definition above refers to the range of motion provided by your muscles. Range of motion is how far your muscles allow a specific joint to move when attempting full flexion and full extension. Stretching is one way to help you move with ease, which translates into getting to and returning balls without pulling anything!

Mobility

mo·bil·i·ty [moh-bil-i-tee], noun

1. The quality or state of being mobile.
2. The ability to move in one's environment with ease and without restriction.[3]

While flexibility refers mainly to the range of motion allowed by the muscles, mobility includes the muscles, joints, joint capsule, and soft tissue surrounding the joints. It's affected by any dysfunction that inhibits your range of motion in a specific joint or group of joints. Flexibility is how far you have the potential to move. Mobility is moving with control and the ability to activate your muscles. The two are forever intertwined.

Here is an example. Extend your arm straight out in front of you and spread your fingers wide apart. Without moving your arm or twisting your hand, make a large circle with your thumb. Feel the muscles in your hand working to make the biggest circle possible.

The **mobility** of your thumb is how well you can activate your muscles and move your thumb through the range of motion without assistance. Now grab your thumb and gently pull it toward your forearm. You can feel some of the muscles stretch, right? This assisted stretch is your **flexibility** of the muscles involved in that movement.

To move well and move athletically on the pickleball court, work for ideal mobility in these joints:

- *spine:* flexion, extension, and rotation
- *hips:* flexion, extension, internal rotation, and external rotation
- *pelvis:* finding and stabilizing in neutral position
- shoulders, wrists, knees, and ankles

You may have limitation in your mobility if you:

- have experienced injuries in the past,
- deal with chronic pain, or
- have had surgery on a joint.

Exercises

The following exercises are building blocks to improve your flexibility, mobility, balance, and stability. As you learn which exercises apply specifically to you, you can incorporate some or all of these into your daily exercise routine. Descriptions and photos of each exercise are also included here. For a video guide, more detailed explanation, and additional stretches, visit https://pickleballbody.com/videos.

Mobility & Flexibility Exercises

- Shoulder Circles
- Neck Mobilization (Left and Right)
- Standing Calf Stretch: Gastrocnemius
- Standing Calf Stretch: Soleus

- Ankle Circles
- Standing Hip Circles
- Moving Groin Stretch
- Downward-Facing Dog
- Facedown Quads Stretch
- Thoracic Rotation from Table Pose

Shoulder Circles

- Stand with neutral posture and hands at your sides.
- Lift both arms out to a *T* with your palms facing forward.
- Circle your shoulders through their entire range of motion at a comfortable pace.
- Pay close attention to keeping your neck and trapezius relaxed. Use them to stabilize your shoulders, but don't flex them or scrunch them up.

- To get maximum benefit from this movement, keep your torso still and avoid twisting.

Neck Mobilization (Left and Right)

- Stand or kneel with neutral spine and your core engaged. Let your arms rest at your sides.

- Keep your shoulders down and back.

- With your mouth closed and eyes even with the horizon (not tilting your head), gently turn your head as far as you can to the right.

- Now, without moving, look as far as you can to the right. Then turn your head a little farther right.

- Hold the new position about 5 seconds, come back to neutral, and repeat on the other side.

- Complete 3–5 repetitions on each side.

Standing Calf Stretch: Gastrocnemius

- Stand facing a sturdy object or wall and place your hands on the object at shoulder level.

- Step your right leg 2 feet back while keeping your chest and belly button facing forward.

- Keep both heels on the floor and your right knee straight. Bend your left knee and move it forward toward the object until you feel the stretch in your right calf.

- Hold for 30–45 seconds. Repeat with the other leg and hold for 30–45 seconds.

Standing Calf Stretch: Soleus

- Stand facing a sturdy object or wall and place your hands on the object at shoulder level.

- Step your right leg 1 foot back while keeping your chest and belly button facing forward.

- While keeping both heels on the floor, bend both knees and move them gently forward toward the object until you feel the stretch in your right calf.

- Hold for 30–45 seconds. Repeat with the other leg and hold for 30–45 seconds.

Ankle Circles

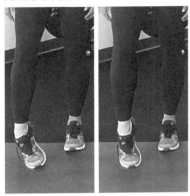

- Stand with neutral posture and hands at your sides. Place your right foot a half step forward.

- Lift your right heel and slowly draw an imaginary clockwise circle with your heel. Feel the muscles of your foot and lower leg activating as you try to make the circle as big as possible.

- Repeat 5 times.

- Draw counterclockwise circles with the same foot.

- Switch feet and repeat.

Standing Hip Circles

- Stand tall with neutral spine and your core engaged.
- Lift one leg off the ground and bend your knee 90 degrees. Keep your other knee soft, not locked.
- Keep your chest and belly button facing forward. Move your knee away from the midline of your body, and draw an imaginary circle in the air with your knee.
- Perform 10 repetitions and then switch directions.
- Switch legs and repeat.

Moving Groin Stretch

- Stand tall with feet wider than shoulder width apart, with neutral spine and your core engaged.

- Keep your toes facing straight ahead.

- While keeping your right leg straight, bend your left knee and lean your body weight onto your left leg.

- Your left heel should be flat on the ground, your hip hinged so your bottom sticks out behind you. Your chest should be facing forward, slightly hinged toward the ground.

- Hold the stretch for 5 seconds. Then bend your right knee, staying low and shifting your body weight to your right leg while straightening the left.

- Hold the stretch for 5 seconds. Repeat.

- Complete 5 repetitions on each side.

Downward-Facing Dog

- Start from a straight arm plank.

- Point your tailbone toward the ceiling and walk your feet slightly toward your hands until you feel a stretch down the back of your legs.

- Keeping your knees fairly straight, gently push your chest toward your thighs while allowing your heels to drop slowly toward the floor. Your heels do not have to touch the ground.

Facedown Quads Stretch

- Lie face down on your exercise mat.

- Reach back with your right hand and grab the toes of your right foot. If you cannot reach your foot, use a band or a towel.

- Pull your right foot as close to your bottom as you can.

- As you feel the stretch in your quad, push your knee toward the back of the room, as far away from your hip as you can. It will not move very far, but this subtle shift will increase the stretch.

- Squeeze your glutes and tuck your bottom under.

- Hold for 45 seconds, then switch to the other side.

Thoracic Rotation from Table Pose

- Start from table pose, with your core engaged to at least 50 percent.

- Raise your right hand and place it below your right ear without leaning to the left. You'll have to use your core to stay centered.

- Try to keep your belly button facing the ground (or mostly toward the ground). Rotate your chest to the right as far as you can without scrunching your neck or pushing too hard off your left hand.

- Hold the position for 3 seconds, then come back to starting position.
- Repeat 8 times.

Take-Home Points

1. Regular stretching and mobility work are key to reducing pain and risk of future injury. Quick fixes won't last long-term!

2. The muscles, bones, and joints in your body are all connected to one another. It's best to work them all to ensure you don't overcompensate and injure yourself.

3. Your flexibility and mobility may be limited at first. They will improve with regular practice.

9

Balance, Coordination & Agility

Imagine you were starting out with a trainer and they asked, "So how's your balance?" You might think, "Well, I haven't fallen down in a while, so my balance is OK. But it could probably be better."

If the subject shifted to your coordination, you might say, "My coordination is decent. I play regular sports." And upon mention of agility, "Hmm, maybe I should know more about this if I'm going to improve as an athlete."

Just as mobility and flexibility are intertwined, so are balance, coordination, and agility. In fact, all the elements of fitness in this section impact one another—for better and for worse.

Balance, coordination, and agility come to us naturally when we're young, so it's easy to take them for granted. As time goes on, we forget about working on balance and coordination. If we ignore these things for too long, even the most talented people will struggle to maintain them as they age. Life obligations, limited time, and lack of a clear path to improve are some reasons people struggle with these elements of fitness.

Thankfully, you have pickleball. Passion for a sport can be the spark that lights the fire to achieve more than you thought possible. No matter what your starting point, whether novice or advanced, you can achieve another level in your athletic endeavors. Balance, coordination, and agility are parts of your journey to improved performance and athleticism. Even if you feel apprehensive because you're not great at them now, it's time to embrace them.

Balance
bal·ance [bal–*uh*ns], noun

1. A state of equilibrium or equipoise; equal distribution of weight, amount, etc.[1]

When you walk, there is a fraction of a second that you are balancing on one foot. During that time, you're performing one of the simplest versions of a balance exercise.

Your ability (or inability) to balance on one foot becomes more important with the stops and starts required in pickleball. Why? Because you are balancing on one leg *a lot* more than you realize. The protective mechanisms of your body and brain do everything they can to prevent you from falling. If you don't have good balance, you will subconsciously slow down so you don't fall. The good news is that by dedicating time to improving your static and dynamic balance, you will move faster and more efficiently—ultimately becoming a better athlete.

Static balance is maintaining equilibrium and control over your center of gravity when you're stationary. Dynamic balance is doing the same while moving. We use our vision, sound (vestibular system), and proprioception (body awareness) to keep our balance.

Your center of gravity is the point around which all your weight is evenly distributed, and its exact location varies from person to person. Your center of gravity shifts as you move or encounter external resistance. Having good balance means having control over your center of gravity while stationary, moving, or encountering resistance. As you improve both types of balance and gain greater control over your center of gravity, you will improve your overall body control. You'll also reduce your risk of injury from awkward movements and falls.

Coordination

co·or·di·na·tion [koh-awr-dn-ey-sh*un*], noun

1. The ability to use different parts of the body together smoothly and efficiently.[2]

Coordination is the ability of muscles to work together voluntarily for purposeful movement. Performing a coordinated movement involves three steps that utilize your brain, nerves, and muscles:

1. You envision the movement you want to perform.

2. Your brain sends nerve signals to your muscles.

3. Your muscles receive these signals and move.

How can coordinated movements assist me with pickleball, you ask? The movements required for a stellar game of pickleball are multipart movements, which include things like:

- turning your hips,

- transferring your body weight,

- using your core to transfer the power from your lower to upper body,

- rotating your upper body,

- moving your arms, and

- maintaining hand-eye coordination.

If it's not obvious already, pickleball requires significant coordination, timing, and body control. When you practice improving your coordination, you'll see the difference in your game.

Agility

a·gil·i·ty [*uh*-jil-i-tee], noun

1. The power of moving quickly and easily; nimbleness.[3]

When you are agile, you can *move and change your direction quickly and in a controlled manner*. Your reflexes are sharp, and you have the coordination, balance, and speed to take information in and respond to it in kind. To improve agility, start with goals to improve flexibility, mobility, balance, and coordination. From there, you can add these agility exercises into your training plan:

- *lateral movement:* moving side to side with speed
- *high knees:* stationary and moving in various directions
- *foot speed drills:* starting with forward/backward movement and shifting to box jumps when appropriate

The ability to change body position quickly and efficiently requires balance and coordination. These skills work together to allow you to be more reactive and quicker. The dynamic stop-start nature of pickleball requires short bursts of energy. You can improve upon these skills with high-intensity speed and agility work. Examples include using a jump rope, cone drills, a treadmill, or a track.

These skills may not be everyone's first area of focus when training to be a better player, as they depend on your current fitness level. But *anyone* can improve their agility, regardless of age. As with any exercise program, make sure you have a doctor's clearance before starting any new type of training. If you have never worked to improve your agility, obtain proper instruction from a trainer or health professional before you begin.

Exercises

The following exercises are building blocks you can use to improve your balance, coordination, and agility. Start by mastering the easy ones, and increase in difficulty as you progress. I've often trained people who think they should try difficult exercises immediately because they could once do them, even if they have not done them for decades. Please consider your own safety and be realistic when starting your agility training. You can improve with training, regardless of your age. But choose the right starting point and progress gradually for success. Descriptions and photos of each exercise are included here. For a video demonstration and additional exercises, visit https://pickleballbody.com/videos.

Balance, Coordination & Agility Exercises

- Single Leg Balance with Assistance
- Single Leg Balance without Assistance (Eyes Open, Eyes Closed)
- Single Leg Balance without Assistance (Limbs in Motion)
- High Knees
- Quick Feet
- Shuffle-Shuffle Touch

Single Leg Balance with Assistance

- Place one hand gently on a table or chair for balance.
- Standing in neutral posture, engage your core by drawing your navel in.
- Focus on a spot on the wall or floor.
- Maintain neutral posture and lift one leg off the ground, with your knee in front of you, until your thigh is parallel to the floor.
- Hold for 45 seconds, then switch legs.
- Use as little assistance as possible.

Single Leg Balance without Assistance
(Eyes Open, Eyes Closed)

- Standing in neutral posture, engage your core by drawing your navel in.

- Focus on a spot on the wall or floor.

- Maintain neutral posture and lift one leg off the ground, with your knee in front of you, until your thigh is parallel to the floor.

- Hold for 45 seconds, then switch legs.

- To further challenge yourself, repeat the exercise with your eyes closed.

- With eyes closed, hold the posture and count down from 10 seconds.

Single Leg Balance without Assistance (Limbs in Motion)

- Standing in neutral posture, engage your core by drawing your navel in.
- Focus on a spot on the wall or floor.
- Maintain neutral posture and lift one leg off the ground, with your knee in front of you, until your thigh is parallel to the floor.

- Straighten your leg in front of you, then slowly kick your leg behind you.

- Bring your leg back beneath you, without touching your foot to the ground.

- Slowly raise the elevated foot out to your side, and then return your leg back underneath you without touching your foot to the ground.

- Repeat this movement for 45 seconds; switch legs.

High Knees

- Standing in neutral posture, engage your core by drawing your navel in.

- Focus on a spot on the wall or floor.

- Maintain neutral posture and lift your right leg off the ground, with your knee in front of you, until your thigh is parallel to the floor.

- Hold for 10 seconds, and quickly place your leg back on the floor, transitioning swiftly to lifting your left leg with your thigh parallel to the floor. Hold for 10 seconds.

- As you improve your balance, you will be able to transition quicker between legs. For increased challenge, hold your elevated leg for less time, and focus on transitioning quickly between each leg.

Quick Feet

- Find a short platform, approximately 2–4 inches tall.

- Facing the platform, with one foot at a time, step at least half of your foot onto the platform. Then step down, leading with the same foot.

- With the goal of increasing your foot speed, start slowly and allow yourself to get into a rhythm. Gradually increase your speed until you are stepping on and off as quickly as you can.

- Repeat for 30 seconds on each foot.

Shuffle-Shuffle Touch

- Set up two markers about 6 feet apart.

- Stand with athletic posture (feet aligned with shoulders, knees bent, sending hips behind you). Line up your right foot with your left marker.

- Shuffle two steps to the right so that your left foot is lined up with the right marker.

- Touch the floor (or marker) by bending your knees while keeping your back straight.

- Return to athletic ready position and shuffle two steps to the left.

- Touch the floor. Repeat in 30-second intervals.

Take-Home Points

1. Improving balance and control over your center of gravity improves your overall body control. It also reduces your risk of injury from falls or improper movement.

2. Incorporating multimuscle, coordinated movements into your workouts will translate to increased coordination on the court—so you can hit the ball where and when you want.

3. Speed exercises such as jumping rope, cone drills, and short sprints allow you to react more quickly on the court.

PART 3

Prevent & Manage Injuries

Story from the Court

If someone had told me five years ago that I would spend my retirement chasing a whiffle ball around a court that has a kitchen you're not supposed to enter (except in a few circumstances), I would have called them crazy. Looks like I'm the crazy one now!

My first foray into pickleball was in 2017 when I was visiting my cousins in Ann Arbor. I wasn't excited about playing. But once I learned the basics of the game—thanks to the patience and kindness of the other player—I was hooked. The minute I got home, I signed up for pickleball lessons, and I've been playing about five days a week ever since.

In January 2021, my elbow started to hurt a lot while I was playing pickleball. Instead of taking a little time off to heal, I bought some elbow braces and kept playing. There were a few days when the pain was so bad, I took ibuprofen just so I could play. Eventually, I got an MRI of my right elbow and found out I had tennis elbow, golf elbow, and a moderately torn tendon. Everything in my pickleball world came to a screeching halt.

I started physical therapy and learned some good exercises and stretches. Initially, my physical therapist would only allow me to play pickleball with my left hand. Try that sometime . . . it's very humbling. Luckily, my daily pickle pals decided to play left-handed as well, so I wasn't the only one at a disadvantage. I was very touched by that. We also had a lot of laughs realizing how terribly uncoordinated we all were playing with our left hands.

The moral of my story is to listen to your body when your elbows, knees, shoulders, or other body parts start to hurt. Deal with them before they take you off the court. Learn some stretches for your specific ailment, and do them faithfully so you can get back to that crazy game we all love!

—Julie Muer, Manhattan Beach, CA

Part 3: Prevent & Manage Injuries

Have you ever had an experience like this?

You've finally gotten into the pickleball league you were hoping for and have a great partner. You signed up for a few tournaments, and you know it's going to be a blast. After a good week at work, you are ready to go away for a long weekend with the family. You've been planning it for months. You stop at a restaurant for lunch. You get out of the car . . . and your back goes out.

You grin and bear it while you do a slow shuffle across the parking lot. You don't want anyone to know just how much pain you feel. But the pain *continues* for the *entire* trip. You are forced to cancel pickleball for the week ahead and sit on the sidelines during vacation.

While sitting around, you realize that you'd been ignoring tightness in your back for weeks. You didn't want to admit it, because then you couldn't play pickleball. Then you might lose your new partner. Or you might not be able to play in the tournaments you planned. You realize your busy schedule and too much sitting at work left no time to stretch or do anything outside pickleball. It finally culminated and pushed your body over the edge.

All you did was get out of the car—and now your back is messed up. Others (and by "others," I mean Sanjay ☺) have had their back go out while brushing their teeth, trying on new slippers, or sleeping on an old mattress. Does any of this sound familiar?

The combined time you spend driving a car, sitting at the computer, hunching over your phone, and slouching have long-term effects on your body. If you add pickleball, or any sport, into the mix without regard for injury prevention strategies, you will probably run into trouble.

Experts estimate 80 percent of people will have back pain at some point during their lives,[1] much of it preventable. I don't want you to be one of them! That's why this section is all about managing and preventing injuries. No, it's not a cure-all, because sports are unpredictable, and we cannot prevent every negative outcome. But with consistency and dedication, you can significantly reduce your risk of aggravating an old injury or experiencing a new one. Try it for a few weeks, and you'll see why these exercises are well worth your time.

10

Improving Upper Body Mobility & Preventing Neck, Shoulder, and Elbow Problems

SANJAY (thinking to himself): Jes is over the top with this shoulder thing . . . I mean, it's not like I'm going to make a medical appointment or ask a colleague about this shoulder stuff she keeps bringing up. It doesn't really hurt that bad . . . And who cares about a little grinding noise?

JES (thinking to herself): Sanjay thinks none of this shoulder stuff matters. I know he's just pretending to be listening. He never does the exercises at home that I tell him to do!

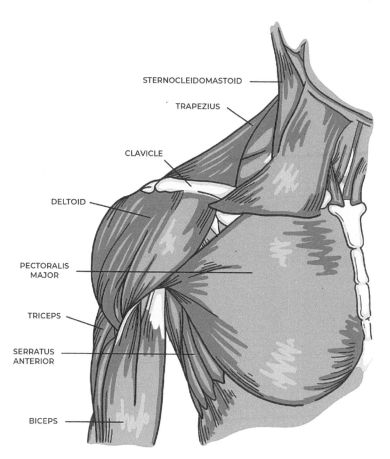

STERNOCLEIDOMASTOID

TRAPEZIUS

CLAVICLE

DELTOID

PECTORALIS
MAJOR

TRICEPS

SERRATUS
ANTERIOR

BICEPS

Seven years later . . .

SANJAY: Hey Jes, the mobility work we've done has really
helped my pickleball game. You've already helped me
with my right shoulder Now I want to improve my left.

Plus, I've noticed many of my pickle pals have shoulder pain that seems to come and go. Why is that? I can't keep taking ibuprofen forever.

JES: Well, thank God for pickleball. Now we can start working on things I want to work on! As for your pickle pals' unpredictably achy shoulders, the repetitive motion of racquet sports often results in tennis elbow or shoulder pain. The racquet motion combined with the common upper body postures many of us have—like slouching while standing, sitting, driving, and using our phones—is a one-two punch to the shoulder and elbow. The two of them combined can strain and cause pain in the joints, ligaments, tendons, and muscles that are already less than perfect.

Repetitive motion from less-than-ideal postures is one thing that can leave us more vulnerable to injury. Old injuries and genetics are two others. You can't change your genetics or go back in time to undo injuries from the past. But you can improve your strength and flexibility and develop a balance of strength throughout your body. This will reduce your risk of new or reinjury and relieve aches and pains that you think you have to "live with." The joy of being pain free or just having less pain is a great motivator to work on upper body mobility.

When most people have pain or discomfort, the immediate reaction is to give direct attention to the area of pain. If the front of your shoulder hurts, you might stretch or ice the front of the shoulder. This may alleviate the acute pain, but the injury could keep coming back or feel sore every time you play.

This approach doesn't work because your upper thoracic spine, neck, shoulders, and elbows are all connected. The imbalances, limitations, or restrictions of one can impact the other. A general term for this is *referred pain*. For pickleball players, upper body mobility issues often manifest as shoulder or elbow pain.

Below are some exercises to address common mobility restrictions that can result in shoulder and elbow pain. Descriptions and photos of each exercise are also included here. For a video demonstration and further details, please see our video at https://pickleballbody.com/videos.

General Upper Body Mobility

Upper Body Mobility Exercises

- Snow Angel on Foam Roller
- Chest Clasp Stretch
- Shoulder Circles
- Kneeling Reach-Over Stretch
- Cat/Cow/Table
- Scapula Protraction/Retraction from Table Pose
- Thoracic Rotation from Table Pose

Snow Angel on Foam Roller (also see Appendix)

- Using a foam roller, lie down lengthwise directly on the roller with your bottom at one end, head at the other, and spine directly over the roller.

- Place your arms out to your sides, making a *T* with your palms up.

- Keeping your arms fairly straight, slowly arch your arms over your head, stopping at brief intervals to feel the stretch.

Chest Clasp Stretch

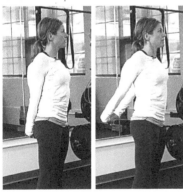

- Stand tall with neutral posture and knees soft.

- Reach behind your back and lace your fingers together.

- Using your laced fingers as leverage, pull your shoulder blades together and open your chest. The sensation should feel like your collar bones are as far apart as possible and your chest and shoulders are being stretched.

- Lift your hands up and away from your bottom if you can, but this is not required. Use the intensity of your stretch as a guide.

Shoulder Circles

- Stand with neutral posture and hands at your sides.

- Lift both arms out to a *T* with your palms facing forward.

- Circle your shoulders through their entire range of motion at a comfortable pace.

- Pay close attention to keeping your neck and trapezius relaxed. Use them to stabilize your shoulders, but don't flex them or scrunch them up.
- To get maximum benefit from this movement, keep your torso still and avoid twisting.

Kneeling Reach-Over Stretch

- Starting on your hands and knees, move your bottom toward your heels while keeping your arms straight.
- With your arms straight out in front of you, you should start to feel a stretch along the sides of your back.
- Move both hands slightly to your right, across the midline of your body. Side bend ever so slightly to feel a stretch on the opposite side.
- Repeat, reaching the other direction.

Cat/Cow/Table

- *Start from table pose:* Get on your hands and knees, making sure your hands are directly below your shoulders and your knees are directly below your hips. Draw your navel in to engage your core.

- *Cat pose:* With your core strongly engaged, slowly tuck your tailbone and round your shoulders, allowing your head to drop down. Slowly transition to cow pose.

- *Cow pose:* Push your shoulders down, lift your chin, and arch your back while keeping your core engaged to at least 50 percent.

- Repeat this sequence 5 times with control and core engagement.

Scapula Protraction/Retraction from Table Pose

- Start from table pose, with your core engaged to at least 50 percent.

- Keeping your elbows straight and your entire back neutral, squeeze your shoulder blades together. Make sure you have a large space between your ears and shoulders while squeezing.

- While maintaining your elbows straight out, ear-to-shoulder space, and neutral spine, push your shoulder blades apart.
- Repeat 15 times at moderate speed, being careful not to engage your neck and trapezius (muscles at the back of the neck and shoulders).

Thoracic Rotation from Table Pose

- Start from table pose, with your core engaged to at least 50 percent.
- Raise your right hand and place it below your right ear without leaning to the left. You'll have to use your core to stay centered.
- Try to keep your belly button facing the ground (or mostly toward the ground). Rotate your chest to the right as far as you can without scrunching your neck or pushing too hard off your left hand.
- Hold the position for 3 seconds, then come back to starting position.
- Repeat 8 times.

Neck Mobility

Note: All neck mobility and stretching should be done with a gentle approach. Start conservatively and listen to your body's cues.

Neck Mobility Exercises

- Ear to Shoulder Stretch
- Chin to Clavicle Stretch
- Double Chin
- Neck Mobilization (Left and Right)

Ear to Shoulder Stretch

- Stand or kneel with neutral spine and your core engaged. Let your arms rest at your sides.

- Keep your shoulders down and back.

- With your mouth closed and eyes straight ahead, slowly tilt your right ear toward your right shoulder.

- Gently push your left shoulder toward the floor by walking your left-hand fingertips down your left leg. Hold for 15 seconds.

- Switch sides by repeating the steps on your other side (left ear to shoulder).

- Alternate sides, for a total of 5 repetitions per side.

Chin to Clavicle Stretch

- Stand or kneel with neutral spine and your core engaged. Let your arms rest at your sides.

- Keep your shoulders down and back.

- With your mouth closed and eyes straight ahead, slowly tilt your right ear toward your right shoulder.

- Turn your chin toward your right collarbone and cast your eyes down toward the floor.

- Hold the stretch for 15–30 seconds.
- Repeat once on the other side.

Double Chin

- Stand or kneel with neutral spine and your core engaged. Let your arms rest at your sides.
- Keep your shoulders down and back.
- With your mouth closed and eyes even with the horizon (not tilting your head), gently draw your chin toward the back of the room so that it feels like you are making a double chin. You should feel gentle activation of the muscles in the back of your head at the base of your skull.
- Hold for 5 seconds, then return to the start position.
- Repeat 5 times.

Neck Mobilization (Left and Right)

- Stand or kneel with neutral spine and your core engaged. Let your arms rest at your sides.

- Keep your shoulders down and back.

- With your mouth closed and eyes even with the horizon (not tilting your head), gently turn your head as far as you can to the right.

- Now, without moving, look as far as you can to the right. Then turn your head a little farther right.

- Hold the new position about 5 seconds, come back to neutral, and repeat on the other side.

- Complete 3–5 repetitions on each side.

Shoulder Mobility

Shoulder Mobility Exercises

- Internal & External Rotation Lying Down Face Up
- Lying Down *T*s, *Y*s, *I*s
- Miniband External Rotator Activation from Kneeling

Internal & External Rotation Lying Down Face Up

- Lie face up on the floor with your knees bent and feet flat on the ground.

- Move your arms so your elbows are straight out from your shoulder, with a 90-degree bend between your elbow and forearm. Your fingers should be pointing upward. Your palms should be facing forward.

- Gently squeeze your shoulder blades together and push your shoulders away from your ears. Move the palm of your hand toward the floor by rotating your upper arm, keeping your shoulder stationary and maintaining the 90-degree bend at the elbow. You do not have to touch the floor with your hands. Simply go as far as you can without pain or compromising form.

- Using the same guidelines, return to starting position and continue to arch the back of your hand to the floor behind you.

- Return to your starting position and repeat 5–10 times, holding each position for 3 seconds.

Lying Down *T*s, *Y*s, *I*s

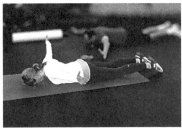

- Lie face down on the floor with your hands out to your sides to create what looks like a giant letter *T*.

- Your palms will be facing forward with your thumbs pointing toward the ceiling like a hitchhiker.

- Try to rotate your elbow crease toward the front of the room.

- While keeping your thumbs pointing toward the ceiling and slightly toward the back of the room, lift your arms slightly off the floor.

- Hold your arms off the floor and make a small pulsing motion toward the ceiling while squeezing the muscles along your upper back and shoulder blades.

- Maintain the *T* position with your arms while pulsing.
- Repeat 10 times with your arms in the *T*, *Y*, and *I* positions.

Miniband External Rotator Activation from Kneeling

- Stand or kneel with neutral spine and your core engaged.
- Choose a moderate-level miniband and put it around your forearms close to your elbows.
- With your hands directly in front of your shoulders, bend your elbows 90 degrees and keep your palms facing forward.
- Pulse your forearms away from each other while keeping them parallel. Keep your shoulders down, far away from your ears and forearms parallel to each other. Your elbows should be directly under your wrists.
- Repeat 10 times with a slow, controlled motion.

Elbow Problems

Elbow Mobility Exercises

- Forearm Flexion & Extension Stretch
- Wrist Flexion & Extension
- Radial & Ulnar Deviation
- Forearm Pronation & Supination

Forearm Flexion & Extension Stretch

- Hold your right arm straight out from your shoulder with your palm facing up and fingers pointing down toward the ground.

- Use your left hand to grasp the fingers of the right and pull the back of the hand toward your body.

- Repeat 3 times, holding for 10 seconds each time. Repeat using your left arm.

- Use the same technique with your palm facing down.

Wrist Flexion & Extension

- Hold your arms straight out in front of you, and make a fist with each hand.

- With your palms down, flex your wrist upward by bringing the back of your hand toward the top of your forearm. Hold the flexion for 5 seconds.

- Return to neutral wrist and without stopping, bring the inside of your palm toward the bottom of your forearm. Hold the flexion for 5 seconds.

- Repeat this motion 10 times.

Radial & Ulnar Deviation

- Hold your arms straight out in front of you, and make a fist with each hand.

- Turn your hands so that your palms are facing each other and your thumbs are facing up. While keeping your forearms stationary, flex your wrists downward and hold for 5 seconds.

- Return your wrists to neutral. Then flex your wrists upward. Hold for 5 seconds.

- Repeat 10 times in each direction.

Forearm Pronation & Supination

- With your arms at your sides straight down from your shoulders, bend your elbows 90 degrees.

- Keep your palms open and your forearms stationary. Rotate your hands from palms up to palms down.

- Repeat 10 times in each direction.

Take-Home Points

1. Regularly engaging in upper body mobility and strength training can reduce your risk of injury from the repetitive motions of pickleball.

2. Upper body, neck, and shoulder mobility is important in keeping you healthy and able to play the game you love.

3. Strength isn't just for the big muscles but also for the small, stabilizing muscles that keep us safe from injury. Develop a balance of strength throughout your body.

11

Improving Hip Mobility & Preventing Lower Back Problems

SANJAY: I remember when I had a herniated disc in my lower back. What a mess. I had a hard time standing for long periods of time at work or bending over to brush my teeth—which is kind of scary. I spent time rehabilitating my back by going to "back school," and it feels great most of the time. Still, I feel a little apprehensive about reinjuring it sometimes. I don't want to go through that again—I don't have time.

JES: Eighty percent of adults will experience an episode of lower back pain in their lives.[1] For some people, the pain is temporary. The injury occurs, they go to their doctor and physical therapy, and they feel better and forget it ever happened. For others, the pain goes to another level. It's hard to endure on a daily basis. Although they've tried many therapies and treatments, the intolerable pain never goes away.

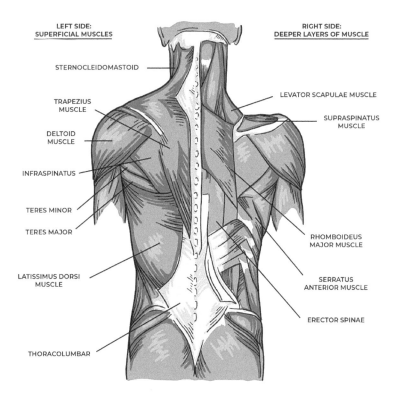

LEFT SIDE:
SUPERFICIAL MUSCLES

RIGHT SIDE:
DEEPER LAYERS OF MUSCLE

STERNOCLEIDOMASTOID

LEVATOR SCAPULAE MUSCLE

TRAPEZIUS
MUSCLE

SUPRASPINATUS
MUSCLE

DELTOID
MUSCLE

INFRASPINATUS

TERES MINOR

TERES MAJOR

RHOMBOIDEUS
MAJOR MUSCLE

LATISSIMUS DORSI
MUSCLE

SERRATUS
ANTERIOR MUSCLE

ERECTOR SPINAE

THORACOLUMBAR

Between the individuals in those two scenarios are those who often have a dull ache in their lower back. The back pain is often worse when they wake up in the morning or after a day of being extremely active. Things like moving furniture and shoveling snow provoke pain that lasts a few days and then slowly fades away. Others may have a constant low-level soreness in their lower backs that they just learn to live with. They take ibuprofen when needed—more often than they should. But many people don't know of any other options for relief.

A consistent, dull backache or occasionally tweaking your back can take low-level, tolerable pain to an almost intolerable level. If this happens to you, these two things could be your solution:

1. Improve the mobility and flexibility of your upper legs and hips.
2. Increase your core strength.

The following exercises and images can assist you with hip flexibility and mobility and core strength. These exercises are a foundation for back care, but they will not cure severe injuries like herniated discs. If you have severe back pain from disc issues or other injuries, consult your physician or physical therapist before beginning any new exercises. For a video guide, more detailed explanation, and additional stretches, visit https://pickleballbody.com/videos.

Hip Mobility

Hip Mobility Exercises

- Standing Hip Circles
- Standing Abduction
- Spiderman Hip Mobility

Standing Hip Circles

- Stand tall with neutral spine and your core engaged.
- Lift one leg off the ground and bend your knee 90 degrees. Keep your other knee soft, not locked.
- Keep your chest and belly button facing forward. Move your knee away from the midline of your body, and draw an imaginary circle in the air with your knee.
- Perform 10 repetitions and then switch directions.
- Switch legs and repeat.

Standing Abduction

- Stand tall with neutral spine and your core engaged.
- Lift one leg off the ground a few inches. Keep your other knee soft, not locked.
- Keep your chest and belly button facing forward, shoulders even and your toes pointing straight ahead. Move your leg out to the side, away from the midline of your body.
- Hold your end range position for 3 seconds, making sure your toes are pointing straight ahead, you are standing upright, and your leg is in the same plane as your body.
- Bring your leg back to starting position with control.
- Perform 10 repetitions and then switch directions.
- Switch legs and repeat.

Spiderman Hip Mobility

- Start from table pose. On your hands and knees, place your hands directly below your shoulders and your knees directly below your hips. Draw your navel in to engage your core.

- Bring your right leg forward, and put your right foot on the ground with your toes next to the base of your right palm (or as close as you can get them).

- Move your left knee back, or if you can, move your left knee back and lift it off the ground. Your toes should still be touching the ground.

- Your body weight will be supported by both hands, your right foot, and the toes on your left foot.

- Using your own leg strength, guide your right knee away from the midline of your body while keeping your foot entirely connected to the ground and your toes pointing straight ahead.

- You will feel this in the inner thigh of your right leg and the front of your left leg.

- Lift your chest so you can look straight ahead.

- Hold for 5 seconds and switch to the other leg.
- Repeat 5 times on each leg.

Glute & Upper Leg

Glute & Upper Leg Stretches

- Moving Groin Stretch
- Kneeling Hip Flexor Stretch
- Downward-Facing Dog
- Seated Glute Stretch
- Facedown Quads Stretch

Moving Groin Stretch

- Stand tall with your feet wider than shoulder width apart, with neutral spine, and with your core engaged.
- Keep your toes facing straight ahead.

- While keeping your right leg straight, bend your left knee and lean your body weight onto your left leg.
- Your left heel should be flat on the ground, your hip hinged so your bottom sticks out behind you. Your chest should be facing forward, slightly hinged toward the ground.
- Hold the stretch for 5 seconds. Then bend your right knee, staying low and shifting your body weight to your right leg while straightening the left.
- Hold the stretch for 5 seconds. Repeat.
- Complete 5 repetitions on each side.

Kneeling Hip Flexor Stretch

- Kneel with one knee down and one knee up.
- Find your neutral pelvic position.
- From neutral, tuck your pelvis slightly under.

- You should feel a stretch in the front of your hip, down through your quad.

- To enhance the stretch, lift the same arm as the kneeling leg overhead. There should be a straight line between your down knee and lifted arm.

Downward-Facing Dog

- Start from a straight arm plank.

- Point your tailbone toward the ceiling and walk your feet slightly toward your hands until you feel a stretch down the back of your legs.

- Keeping your knees fairly straight, gently push your chest toward your thighs while allowing your heels to drop slowly toward the floor. Your heels do not have to touch the ground.

Seated Glute Stretch

- Sit on the ground with both feet out in front of you.

- Cross your right leg over your left so your right knee is bent and your right foot is on the floor above your knee.

- While keeping your chest and belly button facing straight ahead, use your left hand to reach over and grab the outside of your right knee.

- Gently pull your right knee across the midline of your body.

- Be sure you use your right hand to support your body weight and keep yourself sitting extremely straight and tall. If you find yourself leaning back, use a wall or the couch to help keep your spine and pelvis as straight up as possible.

Facedown Quads Stretch

- Lie face down on your exercise mat.

- Reach back with your right hand and grab the toes of your right foot. If you cannot reach your foot, use a band or a towel.

- Pull your right foot as close to your bottom as you can.

- As you feel the stretch in your quad, push your knee toward the back of the room, as far away from your hip as you can. It will not move very far, but this subtle shift will increase the stretch.

- Squeeze your glutes and tuck your bottom under.

- Hold for 45 seconds, then switch to the other side.

Core

As mentioned in chapter 7, "Core & Posture," your core muscles are more than just "six-pack abs." Your core muscles play an important role in your athletic performance and injury prevention. The glutes and core work together to stabilize your lumbar spine and pelvis to protect your lower back. Regular practice of these basic core exercises can work wonders for injury prevention and improved performance. To this day, after decades of training and participating in sports, I still use these simple yet effective exercises on a regular basis. For a video guide, more detailed explanation, and additional stretches, visit https://pickleballbody.com/ videos.

Core Exercises

- Straight Arm and Forearm Plank
- Bilateral Turtle
- Lower Body Hold
- Miniband Glute Bridge
- Miniband Clam Bridge

Straight Arm and Forearm Plank

- The plank trains your muscles to hold neutral spine against outside forces—in this case, gravity. As you get stronger, your muscles will be more capable of protecting your spine during sports and other activities.

- Start from table pose, with your arms directly below your shoulders and your navel drawn in to activate your core.

- Straighten both knees and place both feet on the ground about hip width apart.

- Hold yourself in neutral spine and avoid rounding your upper back, arching your lower back, or holding your hips too high (out of neutral). Think of your ear, shoulder, hip, knee, and ankle being in one straight line, like a plank of wood.

- If you start to feel any discomfort in your lower back, put one knee down but continue to hold neutral spine and activate your core. Even with this modification, the exercise can still be very challenging.

- If you still feel back pain, put both knees down and continue to keep your spine neutral and your core active.

- Try this method from both the straight arm (high plank) and forearm (low plank) position.

- Set a goal of 3 sets of 60-second holds. If you are new to this exercise, start with 15 seconds at a time, rest for 5, and repeat. You'll get stronger quickly when you practice consistently.

Bilateral Turtle

- Lie down on your back with your legs straight.

- Make sure your lower back and pelvis are in a neutral position. Too much of an arch in your lower back or having your hips tilted slightly forward mean you need to tuck your tail under to find neutral.

- Draw your navel in toward your spine to activate your core muscles.

- Lift your left leg off the floor, keeping your knee bent 90 degrees.

- Place your right hand on your left thigh just above your left knee.

- Keeping your right arm straight and your lower back neutral, drive your left knee up, and use your right arm to resist the force.

- You will feel your core muscles—especially around your belly button—as you hold for 5 seconds.

- Switch sides and repeat. Complete 5 repetitions of 5 seconds each.

Lower Body Hold

The **lower body hold** helps you connect with and recruit the muscles in your lower core and pelvic floor. Even though this exercise seems simple, it can dramatically improve your overall core strength. Many of us have a limited ability to intentionally recruit these muscles. The more you practice isometric holds like this one, the better you will be able to access these muscles during activities like pickleball!

- Lie down on your back with your knees bent and feet flat on the floor. Make sure your lower back and pelvis are in a neutral position. Too much of an arch in your lower back or your hips being tilted slightly forward mean you need to tuck your tail under to find neutral.

- Draw your navel in toward your spine to activate your core muscles.

- Lift one leg off the floor, keeping your knee bent at 90 degrees.

- If you can maintain your neutral lower back with one leg off the ground, lift the second leg off the ground. This is what I call the "base" position for the exercise.

- Make sure your core is active and your lower back is neutral. If they are, slowly straighten your knees until you feel the lower part of your core being challenged. Don't allow your back to move.

- Hold your legs at an angle that challenges your core for 60 seconds. Every 10 seconds, try to recruit 10 percent more of your core muscles. Pretend you're at a flexing contest at the beach, and whoever works the hardest wins!

- Some people will find this exercise quite challenging. Others will be tempted to straighten their legs and lower their feet to just above the ground. Rest assured—you do not need to lower your legs extremely close to the ground for this exercise to be effective. In fact, I recommend lowering them only as far as you need to feel your core engage. Then focus on recruiting 10 percent more every 10 seconds from a stationary position.

Miniband Glute Bridge

- Using a miniband of moderate to high difficulty, place the band around your thighs, just above your knees.

- Lie down on your back with your knees bent and feet flat on the floor. Make sure your lower back and pelvis are in a neutral position. Too much of an arch in your lower back or your hips being tilted slightly forward mean you need to tuck your tail under to find neutral.

- Draw your navel in toward your spine to activate your core muscles.

- Place your feet shoulder width apart and lift your toes off the ground.

- Push through your heels and lift your hips off the ground while driving your knees out against the resistance of the miniband. You will feel your glute muscles activating.

- Make sure your lower back is staying neutral.

- Hold for 30 seconds. Come down for a 5-second rest and repeat for at least 3 total bridges.

Miniband Clam Bridge

- Using a miniband of moderate to high difficulty, place the band around your thighs, just above your knees.

- Lie down on your back with your knees bent and feet flat on the floor. Make sure your lower back and pelvis are in a neutral position. Too much of an arch in your lower back or your hips being tilted slightly forward mean you need to tuck your tail under to find neutral.

- Draw your navel in toward your spine to activate your core muscles.

- Keep your feet and knees together. Push through your heels and lift your hips off the ground to create a bridge with your feet and knees together.

- From bridge position, make sure your lower back is in neutral. Then, while keeping your feet fully on the ground, drive your knees out against the resistance of the band.

- Hold for 3 seconds at your end range. Make sure the inside of your foot is still on the ground.

- Repeat 10 times.

Take-Home Points

1. The lower back is a common area for chronic pain, though the causes often begin elsewhere.
2. Improving hip and leg mobility and flexibility, along with building a strong core, will provide a stable base to protect your lower back.

12

Preventing Hamstring, Quadriceps, IT Band & Knee Problems

SANJAY: I'm glad I'm way past my tennis days. Covering that large court and moving that quickly while playing singles is hard on the knees! I don't have to worry about that so much with pickleball, especially when playing doubles. But I still get some discomfort in my hamstrings after playing several hours of pickleball. This is especially true when I play even an hour of singles in pickleball. It reminds me of playing tennis with the constant short-distance sprinting and stretching to reach the ball.

JES: Well, it's true that in tennis you have to cover much more court. But you are still starting, stopping, turning, and lunging for the ball when you play pickleball, no? And if you've had issues with your knees or hamstrings in the past, stretching and mobility work is well worth your time. I think you might be surprised at how regular mobility work can improve your game and reduce or prevent pain.

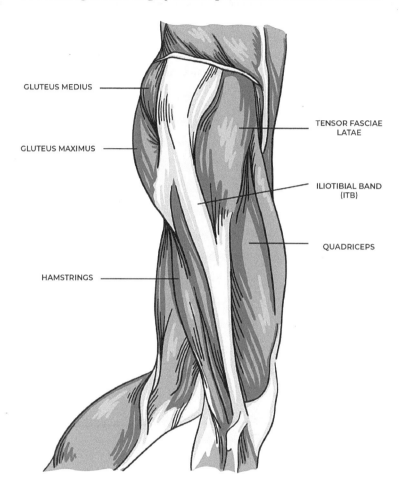

GLUTEUS MEDIUS

GLUTEUS MAXIMUS

HAMSTRINGS

TENSOR FASCIAE LATAE

ILIOTIBIAL BAND (ITB)

QUADRICEPS

Tightness and imbalance in the muscles above your knee can lead to injury. This is often caused by limited hip and/or ankle mobility, improper motor recruitment and patterning, or genetics. Here, we focus on stretches and rolling techniques to keep your hamstrings, quadriceps (quads), and IT band in good working order.

Combining these exercises with hip and ankle mobility and basic strength exercises is the best way to prevent problems. Try these exercises for a few minutes each day and see if you notice any improvements. For a video guide, more detailed explanation, and additional stretches, visit https://pickleballbody.com/videos.

Hamstring, Quadriceps & Iliotibial Band

Hamstring, Quadriceps & IT Band Exercises

- Foam Roll Quad
- Forward Fold IT Band Stretch
- Standing Hamstring Stretch with Hands Behind the Back
- Standing Hamstring Stretch: Single Leg
- Standing Quads Stretch

Foam Roll Quads (also see Appendix)

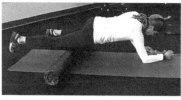

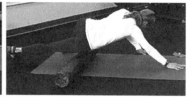

- Lie face down with the roller at the top of your right hip. The roller should be placed between the ground and your body. Rest your upper body on your forearms and elbows.

- Keep your quads as relaxed as possible and toes pointing straight down. Use your arms and left leg to roll the roller down the length of your thigh, stopping just above your knee.

- Repeat 3–5 times, stopping on any tight spots and relaxing the muscles around the tight areas.

- Turn your knee and toes outward away from the midline of your body and roll 3–5 times.

- Move the roller to just above your knee. Turn your knee and toes inward toward the midline of your body and roll the inner, lower two-thirds of your quadriceps.

Forward Fold IT Band Stretch

- Stand with neutral posture with your hands at your sides.
- Cross your left leg behind your right leg.
- Using both hands and keeping your legs straight, fold forward at your waist, reaching your hands toward your back (left) leg.
- If you feel off-balance, use a prop for your hands so you do not have to bend down as far.
- Repeat the exercise with your right leg crossed behind your left.

Standing Hamstring Stretch with Hands Behind the Back

- Stand with neutral posture and place your feet slightly wider than shoulder width apart.

- Place your hands behind your back, and open your chest by squeezing your shoulder blades slightly together. Tighten your core.

- With your body weight in your heels and maintaining neutral spine, hinge at the waist until you feel a stretch in your hamstrings (back of thighs).

- Keep your legs straight without locking your knees.

- You can perform the stretch reaching your chest down the center of your body, leaning toward your right leg, and leaning toward your left leg to enhance the stretch.

Standing Hamstring Stretch: Single Leg

- You can use a chair or countertop to support your balance during this exercise if needed.

- Extend your left leg out about 8–12 inches in front of you. Keep your knee straight and heel down as you lift your toes off the ground.
- Bend forward at your hips and move your bottom toward the back of the room, bringing your chest toward your thigh while keeping your back straight.
- Bend your right leg at the knee.
- Go only as far as you can without feeling a strain.

Standing Quads Stretch

- Stand with neutral posture and place one hand on a stable source of support.
- Bending at the knee, lift one leg off the ground.
- With your hand, grab your lifted foot and bring it up behind you, as if to kick yourself in the bottom.
- Hold this position for 45 seconds and switch legs.

- If you cannot reach your foot with your hand, use a stretch strap or towel to perform the stretch.

Knee

Knee issues are common and arise for many reasons. Causes of knee injuries and pain include poor mechanics, limited hip and ankle mobility, strength imbalances, and over-use. There's no simple answer for knee pain. Many people have experienced ACL and meniscus repairs, arthritis, knee replacements, bursitis, and everything in between. Not to mention, it can be challenging to feel confident about your knees after an injury. But it doesn't have to stop you!

The first step to knee care is understanding why they hurt or were injured in the first place. Sometimes your health care provider will have a great explanation. Other times, injuries and achiness might occur without an obvious cause. Ask questions and get as much information as you can about what may have caused your injury or chronic pain. This information tells you how to focus your efforts and make the best use of your time.

This is by no means an exhaustive resource for all pos-sible knee injuries. It is meant to be a place for you to start and build upon. In this section, we establish the foundation for strengthening the muscles around the knees with basic exercises. Combining strength exercises with the exercises listed in the section above can alleviate achy knees and pro-vide protection from injury.

If you want to progress beyond the exercises listed here, you most certainly can. Work with a professional trainer or physical therapist who takes a whole-body approach. They can help you improve based on your individual needs.

Strength Exercises for Muscles around the Knee

- Wall Sit
- Hamstring Ball Curl
- Squats Using a Miniband
- Calf Raises
- Bridge Heel Walk Outs
- Ball of Foot Push Offs

Wall Sit

- Stand against a strong wall. Face forward with neutral posture and hands at your sides.

- Keeping your back against the wall, walk your feet forward about 12–14 inches. Bend your knees as you lower your bottom down toward the floor.

- Lower yourself down until your knees are bent 45 degrees and your thighs are halfway to parallel. If that feels OK on your joints, continue down to a 90-degree knee bend and parallel thighs. It will look like you are sitting in an imaginary chair.

- Push through your feet from heel to toe, not just in your toes! You will feel your quads working.

- If you have knee pain, bring yourself up a little and move your feet out a little. Try to find a position that challenges your quads without causing pain in your knees.

- Hold for 45–60 seconds.

Hamstring Ball Curl

- Lie down on a mat, face up.

- Place an exercise ball of medium size under your heels and half your calves. Your feet should be about 4–6 inches apart.

- Activate your core and keep your palms down on the floor.
- Dig your heels into the ball and lift your bottom off the floor.
- Bend your knees and pull the ball in toward your bottom. Hold for 1 second.
- Straighten your knees and hold again for 1 second.
- Repeat 15 times.

Squats Using a Miniband

- Stand with neutral posture with your hands at your sides. Have a chair or table nearby in case you need help with balance.
- Using a miniband of moderate to high difficulty, place the band around your thighs, just above your knees.
- Place your feet shoulder width apart and point your toes slightly away from one another.

- With 60 percent of your body weight in your heels and your core strong, simultaneously bend your knees and move your bottom toward the back of the room. It should feel like you are going to sit on a chair that is slightly too far away.

- Push your knees out against the resistance of the miniband.

- Go as low as you can without pain or until your thighs are parallel to the floor, keeping your knees even with or behind your toes. Your eyes and chest should face forward and slightly down.

Calf Raises

- Stand with neutral posture with your hands at your sides.

- Shift your body weight onto the balls of your feet and lift your heels off the ground as high as you can.

- Hold for 1–3 seconds and repeat 12 times.

- You can also do this exercise one foot at a time.

Bridge Heel Walk Outs

- Lie down on a mat, face up. Keep your feet hip width apart. Engage your core by drawing your navel inward toward your spine.

- Bend your knees and walk your feet toward your bottom until your heel is directly below your knee.

- Lift your toes and push your heels into the ground. Lift your bottom off the ground. While maintaining your bridge, move your feet away from your bottom by taking baby steps with your heels.

- You should feel your calves and hamstrings activating.

- If you start to feel cramping, pause and either set your bottom down or reverse the direction of your walk.

Ball of Foot Push Offs

- Perform this exercise slowly, especially if you have experienced sore knees, chronic knee pain, or injuries.

- Stand with neutral posture with your hands at your sides.

- Take a large step back with your right foot, and bend both knees about 45 degrees. Keep your body weight evenly distributed between your front and back legs. This will look and feel similar to a lunge step.

- Keep your left knee directly over your left heel and about half of your body weight on the ball of your left foot.

- Lift your left heel off the ground as high as you can and hold 1–3 seconds. Repeat 10 times.

- If the exercise feels easy and you do not have pain, shift your left knee slightly in front of your left heel and repeat the exercise. Start with a small forward shift, maybe just a quarter inch, and progress slowly. Your ability to move your knee forward and correctly perform the exercise will depend on your ankle and knee mobility and knee strength.

- Repeat the process with your right leg forward. Complete 10 reps in each position.

Take-Home Points

1. Pickleball may use a small court, but quick starts, stops, and lunges are required. Train the muscles that allow for these motions.

2. Tight upper and lower leg muscles can contribute to knee pain and eventual damage. To prevent this, improve mobility and flexibility in your quadriceps, hamstrings, calves, and ankles.

3. Along with regular mobility work, strengthen your leg muscles to better support game play.

13

Preventing Calf, Achilles, and Ankle Problems & Managing Plantar Fasciitis

SANJAY: OK, OK, wearing two tube socks won't solve my foot problems. Supportive shoes, arch supports, and stretching my foot using a roller do seem to help. I get it now. But Jes, speaking of foot and ankle problems—I know so many pickleballers who have torn or strained their Achilles! I've seen it happen. I mentioned it to my coworker the other day, and she said her family member had the same problem. What's up with that? Why is this so common in pickleball?

JES: Here's the thing. When it comes to injuries, athletes of every age are susceptible. One of my friends, a former college volleyball player, still in her 20s, just tore her Achilles while backpedaling during a volleyball game.

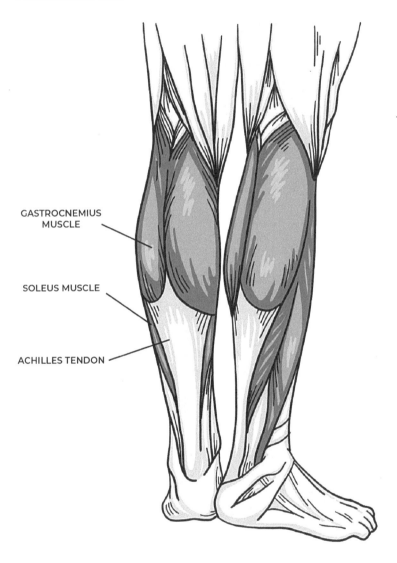

GASTROCNEMIUS
MUSCLE

SOLEUS MUSCLE

ACHILLES TENDON

She had no warning. Side note: she does not work out, stretch, or do mobility work.

When you play sports, there is always some risk of injury because you are in an unpredictable environment. That is the nature of sports, and injuries are part of that unpredictability.

When you're young, the risk for injuries is lower. Yes, because you are young but also because you move, exercise, and stretch more in your youth. Think about it. A kid playing any sport three to five times a week probably has a coach and organized practice sessions during which they stretch and do pertinent drills.

As adults, most of us sit more and move less. You likely won't spend your free time stretching and doing mobility exercises when you can play pickleball instead. This drives your risk up a bit. Plus, you're older and your body isn't what it once was. Many adults don't work on mobility, stretching, and strength. So when you start new activities, your joints, ligaments, and tendons are less prepared to respond.

Picture a former college football player in his late 50s. He hasn't stretched in years. He's busy and cannot justify investing time in stretching and mobility. Let's be honest: it isn't that fun unless you're a fitness nerd like me. Plus, he wouldn't know where to start. That's OK. He's not worried—it's just pickleball.

He plays for a few months and "randomly" tears his Achilles while playing one day. Why? Because even though he's smart, successful, and a former college athlete, he doesn't know anything about ankle mobility or tight calves, quads, and hip flexors. He doesn't know how to deal with glutes that don't fire and how to give his ligaments and tendons the attention they need. To make them perform like the good old days takes work!

Pickleball is a sport for everyone, but it still comes with the uncertainty of any sport. Competitiveness combined with lots of starts, stops, cuts, lunges, and turns put quite the demand on your lower legs, ankles, and feet. So you need those ankles, calves, and feet to be healthy! Many people don't know how to prepare the body for this kind of movement. And many more aren't motivated to spend the time to keep their bodies performing well. These are the main reasons Achilles injuries happen in pickleball.

The exercises listed in this chapter will help you prevent such injuries. Follow along with the images provided or watch a video demonstration at https://pickleballbody .com/videos.

As we've talked about, in the body, all things are connected. Remember that your body has its own limitations. Some people have flat feet or limited mobility in their ankles. Mobility exercises won't fix that. But we can do the work to manage the circumstances we're in.

Calf, Achilles, and Ankle Plantar Fasciitis Problems

Calf, Achilles, and Ankle Plantar Fasciitis Exercises

- Standing Calf Stretch: Gastrocnemius
- Standing Calf Stretch: Soleus
- Foam Roll Calves
- Seated Ankle Circles
- Towel Toe Scrunches
- Foot Roll Out
- Stair Calf Stretch

Standing Calf Stretch: Gastrocnemius

- Stand facing a wall and place your hands on the wall at shoulder level.

- Step your right leg 2 feet back while keeping your chest and belly button facing forward.

- Keep both heels on the floor and your right knee straight. Bend your left knee and move it forward toward the wall until you feel the stretch in your right calf.

- Hold for 30–45 seconds. Repeat with the other leg and hold for 30–45 seconds.

Standing Calf Stretch: Soleus

- Stand facing a wall and place your hands on the wall at shoulder level.

- Step your right leg 1 foot back while keeping your chest and belly button facing forward.

- While keeping both heels on the floor, bend both knees and move them gently forward toward the wall until you feel the stretch in your right calf.

- Hold for 30–45 seconds. Repeat with the other leg and hold for 30–45 seconds.

Foam Roll Calves (also see Appendix)

- You will need a foam roller for this exercise.

- Sitting on the floor, place your right leg on the roller above your ankle.

- Keep your calf relaxed. Your foot should be dangling. Lift your bottom off the ground and roll from above your ankle to below your knee, the length of your calf.

- Repeat 3 times.

- Staying on the same leg and relaxing your calf, rotate your knee and toes inward toward the midline of your body. Roll the inner portion of your calf 3 times

- On the same leg, with a relaxed calf, rotate your knee and toes away from the midline of your body. Roll the outer portion of the length of your calf 3 times.
- Switch legs and repeat.

Seated Ankle Circles

- You will need a foam roller for this exercise.
- Sitting on the floor, place your right leg on the roller above your ankle.
- Slowly draw an imaginary clockwise circle with your big toe. Feel the muscles of your foot and lower leg activating as you try to make the circle as big as possible.
- Repeat 5 times.
- Draw counterclockwise circles with the same foot.
- Switch feet and repeat.

Towel Toe Scrunches

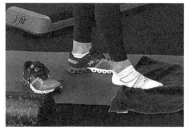

- For this exercise, remove your shoes. You may be barefoot or wear socks.

- You will need a medium-sized towel for this exercise.

- Place the towel under one of your feet.

- Grab the towel with your toes and pull it in toward you, crunching it under your feet.

- Repeat as many times as you can before the towel gets too bunched up.

- Then use your toes to push the towel away from your foot.

- Perform about 8 scrunches and 8 unscrunches.

- Switch feet.

- Repeat 3 times for each foot.

Foot Roll Out

- For this exercise, remove your shoes. You may be bare-foot or wear socks. You will need either a pokey plantar fasciitis ball, a tennis ball, a frozen water bottle, or a rolling pin for this exercise.

- Sit tall on the edge of a chair with neutral posture.

- Place one of the above-mentioned objects under your foot.

- Roll along the length of your foot, starting at the heel and applying pressure as you go, massaging the entire length of your foot from every angle.

- Roll for about 45 seconds and then switch feet.

- Use as much pressure as you feel comfortable using. If you want to add pressure, stand and repeat the process. If standing, hold on to a sturdy object to help you balance.

Stair Calf Stretch

- Find a step or elevated surface that can safely support your body weight. Have something to hold on to for balance and safety.

- Stand on the step with your left foot supporting your body weight and the ball of your right foot at the edge of the step. Your right heel should be hanging over the edge of the elevated surface.

- Keeping your knee straight, exhale and relax your right calf muscle. Slowly let your right heel drop below the level of the step.

- You should feel a gentle stretch from the bottom of your right foot up the back of your leg and to the back of your knee.

- Hold for 30–45 seconds. Switch legs and repeat.

Take-Home Points

1. Not every mobility limitation can be fixed with training, stretching, and strengthening, but many can. Work to improve, and if you sense an issue, consult a health professional. You might be surprised at the progress you can make regardless of age.

2. Investing time to work the joints, tendons, and muscles that support your lower legs and ankles can help prevent many "random" injuries.

3. Be honest with yourself about your current fitness level when you start exercising. It's OK to start slow!

14

Preventing Falls
& Eye Injuries

SANJAY: I was surprised to see eye and wrist injuries due
to falls happening on the court, but I've noticed they're
fairly common. I heard about a pro player who suffered
an eye injury in a national championship game! If you had
asked me before, I would have thought wearing eyewear
was a little over the top.

JES: If you want to prevent eye injuries, the best thing to
do is to *wear eye protection*. Also, working on your balance and coordination regularly wouldn't hurt—both of
these things would improve your reaction time. In my
experience, falls and eye injuries happen for a few reasons. Some are missteps or unexplained accidental falls,
which can happen in any sport, to any player. Falls and
eye injuries can also be the result of poor balance, lack
of body awareness, and reduced reaction time.

SANJAY: Our family went on a wellness retreat where all of
us climbed up a pole and had to balance on it. It was
called "Leap of Faith." We, of course, were harnessed, so

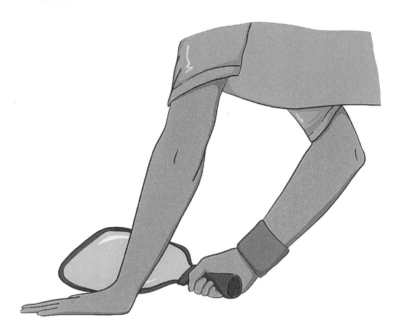

we couldn't free fall. Most of the people in the group—including my wife and kids—got up on the pole and balanced themselves for 30 seconds or more before jumping off. I was an outlier. While I got up on the pole and could stand, I lasted about a nanosecond before falling off. What do I need to work on so I can stay on longer the next time I attempt the "Leap of Faith"?

With time and the right approach, you can improve your balance and coordination, regardless of your age or fitness level. The following exercises can help you improve your balance and coordination. For video demonstrations, please see https://pickleballbody.com/videos.

Beginner Balance & Stability

Beginner Balance Exercises

- Single Leg Balance with Assistance
- Single Leg Balance without Assistance (Eyes Open, Eyes Closed)
- Alternating Single Leg Knee-to-Chest Tucks
- Heel-to-Toe Walk (Forward & Backward)

Single Leg Balance with Assistance

- Place one hand gently on a table or chair.
- Standing in neutral posture, engage your core by drawing your navel in.

- Focus on a spot on the wall or floor.
- Maintain neutral posture and lift one leg off the ground, with your knee in front of you, until your thigh is parallel to the floor.
- Hold for 45 seconds, then switch legs.
- Use as little assistance as possible.

Single Leg Balance without Assistance
(Eyes Open, Eyes Closed)

- Standing in neutral posture, engage your core by drawing your navel in.
- Focus on a spot on the wall or floor.
- Maintain neutral posture and lift one leg off the ground, with your knee in front of you, until your thigh is parallel to the floor.
- Hold for 45 seconds; switch legs.

- To further challenge yourself, repeat the exercise with your eyes closed.

- With your eyes closed, hold your posture and count down from 10 seconds.

Alternating Single Leg Knee-to-Chest Tucks

- Standing in neutral posture, engage your core by drawing your navel in.

- Maintain neutral posture and lift your right leg off the ground, with your knee in front of you, drawing your knee toward your chest.

- Grasp your leg gently with both hands.

- Hold for 10 seconds, and quickly place your leg back on the floor, transitioning swiftly to lifting your left leg. Hold for 10 seconds and maintain balance.

- Repeat 5 times for each leg. As you improve your balance, you will be able to transition quicker between legs.

Heel-to-Toe Walk (Forward & Backward)

  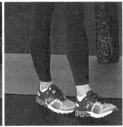

- Find a straight line to use as a reference.
- Stand in neutral posture and engage your core by drawing your navel in.
- Maintain neutral posture and put one foot in front of the other with your heel down and toes up. The heel of your moving foot should touch the toe of your stationary foot. Roll your lifted toes down to touch the ground.
- Next, take the foot that is behind and repeat the motion, placing heel to toe. Lower your toes down to the ground.
- Repeat for 10 steps forward and 10 steps backward.
- When stepping backward, place your toes down behind your heel, and slowly roll your heel down to the ground.

Intermediate Balance & Stability

Intermediate Balance Exercises

- Drinking Bird
- Half–Hip Hinge with Rotation

Drinking Bird

- Stand in neutral posture and engage your core by drawing your navel in.

- Maintain neutral posture and bend one knee 90 degrees, lifting your foot behind you.

- While keeping the knee soft in your supporting leg, hinge at your hip. Move your bottom back and your chest forward toward the floor.

- Extend your arms out in front of you. Stretch out your lifted leg. Keep 70 percent of your weight in the heel of your supporting foot.

- Hold the down position for 5 seconds.

- Return to standing.

- Repeat 5 times for each leg.

Half-Hip Hinge with Rotation

- Stand in neutral posture and engage your core by drawing your navel in.

- Maintain neutral posture and bend one knee 90 degrees, lifting your foot behind you.

- While keeping the knee soft in your supporting leg, hinge at your hip. Move your bottom back and your chest forward toward the floor about 45 degrees, keeping your back straight.

- Let your arms dangle in front of you toward the ground.

- Rotate your chest and arms to the right and hold for 3 seconds.

- Rotate your chest and arms to the left and hold for 3 seconds.

- Repeat 5 times in each direction. For additional stability, hold on to a sturdy object while you rotate side to side.

Coordination

Simple Coordination Exercises

- Quick Feet
- Shuffle-Shuffle Touch

Quick Feet

- Find a short platform, approximately 2–4 inches tall.

- Facing the platform, with each foot, step at least half of your foot onto the platform. Then step down, leading with the same foot.

- With the goal of increasing your foot speed, start slowly and allow yourself to get into a rhythm. Gradually increase your speed until you are stepping on and off as quickly as you can.

- Repeat for 30 seconds on each foot.

Shuffle-Shuffle Touch

- Set up two markers about 6 feet apart.
- Stand with athletic posture, with your right foot lined up with your left marker.
- Shuffle two steps to the right so that your left foot is lined up with the right marker.
- Touch the floor (or marker) by bending your knees while keeping your back straight.
- Return to athletic ready position and shuffle two steps to the left.
- Touch the floor. Repeat in 30-second intervals.

Take-Home Points

1. Proper athletic eyewear prevents most pickleball–associated eye injuries.

2. Balance and coordination are important for both performance and preventing injury. Improving these skills will help you avoid injuries from awkward falls (or near falls).

3. Consistent practice is key. Don't forget to increase the difficulty as your skills improve.

PART 4

Pre- and Postgame Routines & Recovery

Story from the Court

I started playing pickleball over five years ago at a local rec center. At first, I thought it was just an odd thing that older people did. I quickly began to like it a lot and found younger, more athletic people playing it as well. At the time, I was still playing hockey and tennis, but both were getting harder to do without aches. I have now found a competitive-play group and play in a few tournaments a year (if there is no active plague).

From my hockey and singles tennis days, I knew that one needed to train in order to play. Early on, I noticed that I was fitter and played better if I trained outside of the pickleball court. This training included using the elliptical and doing other exercises two to three times a week, about an hour each session. Over time, it seems that I've been playing more (sometimes every day) and training less. This is a mistake. I now realize that training more and playing less is necessary to prevent injury. I'd say that mobility, flexibility, and cardio—in that order—is the best recipe, at least for me.

Pickleball sessions are sometimes casual but can be competitive. If casual, I usually just bounce around a bit, try to get loose, and start playing. I know that I might not go all out for a couple games. If competitive, especially in a tournament, I try to get ready to run hard and chase the ball right from the start. This means 10–15 minutes or more of quick sprints and active stretching and moving, with emphasis on my lower back and hips. I want to break a sweat and feel comfortable running to hit a ball before play begins.

One of the most challenging issues of tournament play is staying warm and loose between games. I have noticed that as I get older, it's easy to lose the sweat and cool down too quickly between games. To avoid stiffening up, I usually put my whole sweat suit back on and try to avoid sitting still. If the wait is too long, I need to repeat my warm-up.

—*Mark Kielb, Ann Arbor, MI*

Part 4: Pre- and Postgame Routines & Recovery

I (Jes) once took an hour-long yoga class before playing in my weekly volleyball league. I was planning on making yoga part of my regular pregame routine. The time and location matched up perfectly with my schedule. It was so convenient, and I knew I needed to add more flexibility work into my fitness regimen. I left the yoga class feeling amazing. I felt loose and mentally relaxed.

What happened next was a shock.

I was so relaxed that my play that night was terrible. I could not react well or anticipate the ball. Honestly, I'm surprised I didn't get hit in the face. And it wasn't just my mind—it was also my body. While I was 100 percent capable of making plays, reacting to the ball, and moving quickly, my body was three steps behind and would not cooperate.

Once I started playing, I knew what had happened. Too much passive stretching before competing was the problem. I should have planned differently, but my ego was in charge. I did not think it would impact my performance. Wrong! Sure, I felt great mentally and physically from holding extreme stretches while breathing. But that level of relaxation is not helpful when you need reactivity and alertness for a competition.

I was in the zone of mental and physical relaxation and experienced poor performance. This is an extreme example of why we need dynamic stretching before a competition and passive stretching afterward. Don't get me wrong, doing a few static stretches for 45 seconds each will not ruin your performance. But as fitness and sport sciences have evolved, we've learned that the timing and type of mobility and stretching matters.

In the next section, I've outlined some helpful ways for you to prep for pickleball, even when you're short on time.

15

Pregame
Warm-Up Routines

SANJAY: I was running late for my pickleball game this weekend and didn't have time to go through my full warm-up
routine. I stretched once or twice and then got on the
court. Wow, am I feeling the effects from that decision.
Jes, what can I do when I don't have a lot of time to
warm up? I'd love to always have 20 minutes to be fully
stretched and ready, but that's not always practical.

JES: If I'm being honest, I do not always warm up before
playing sports or running. But you know what I think to
myself when I choose not to warm up? "You are being
stupid!" And if I really want to win or perform well, I say
it five more times—because I know beyond a shadow of a
doubt that during my first 5 or maybe even 10 plays, I'll be
in "warm-up" mode instead of "top performance" mode.

SANJAY: Oh! Like Mark said earlier?

JES: Exactly. That's just how our bodies work. The nerves
need to be prepped to send signals to the muscles and
joints. And the muscles and joints need blood flow so they

can work at their best. This is especially true for adults who spend most of the day sitting. The physical demand of sitting is so low that it works against our efforts to become better at sports or any type of exercise.

But telling myself "you're being stupid" usually isn't enough to make me change my decision, be smart, and take care of myself by warming up. You know what is? Spraining my ankle because I didn't warm up. I just started playing as soon as I got my shoes on! Getting hurt is a surefire way to make sure I choose differently in the future.

If I find myself starting to think, "I'm a trainer, so I don't need to warm up," I use one of my "trainer mind tricks." Anytime I start sliding into "no warm-up mode," I say to myself, "Remember that time in high school when I tried to jump as high as I could to touch the vaulted ceiling at home? Remember how it was in the middle of winter after just sitting for a while on the school bus? What happened when I landed? I tweaked my back. And why did that happen? Because I wasn't warmed up!" It usually does the trick, because I was only 14 years old when I did that. If that can happen at 14, it can definitely happen as an adult!

The current best practice is to perform a **dynamic warm-up** before a competition. Dynamic warm-ups take your muscles and joints through their range of motion. They send blood flow to your muscles and activate them, so they are ready to perform. You can also foam roll for a few minutes with a focus on improving blood flow to the muscles. After you play, you can foam roll while focusing on releasing deep soreness and tension in the tissue.

Try to warm up for **at least 15 minutes** before you play. But if you are trying to perform at your best, allow for even more time. Warm-ups should include dynamic movement, some easy serves, and a few rallies, gradually increasing in intensity. Sometimes there's a delicate balance between warming up and tiring yourself out. Listen to your body's signals.

The following warm-up routines vary in time requirement from 2 minutes to 15. Following the listed routines, you'll find step-by-step descriptions and images of each exercise. For video demonstrations of these exercises, or for further info, visit https://pickleballbody.com/videos.

SANJAY: Jes, what if I have only two minutes before playing? What should I do to warm up?

JES: Oh my gosh! Did you not listen to what I just said? Fine. For a two-minute warm-up, which is basically *not* warming up, here is what I would do:

2-Minute Warm-Up

• *Dynamic Leg Swings:* 5 forward/backward, 5 side to side

• *Standing Hip Circles:* 5 each direction

• *Torso Rotations:* 10 each direction

SANJAY: What about 5 minutes?

JES: [Eye roll].

5-Minute Warm-Up
- *Dynamic Leg Swings:* 5 forward/backward, 5 side to side
- *Standing Hip Circles:* 5 each direction
- *Torso Rotations:* 8 each direction
- *Dynamic Side Bends:* 5 each direction
- *Shoulder Circles:* 10 each direction
- *Calf Raises:* 10 repetitions

SANJAY: What would a 10–15-minute warm-up include?

JES: Now we're talking!

10–15 Minute Warm-Up
- *Dynamic Leg Swings:* 5 forward/backward, 5 side to side
- *Standing Hip Circles:* 5 each direction
- *Torso Rotations:* 8 each direction
- *Dynamic Side Bends:* 5 each direction
- *Shoulder Circles:* 10 each direction
- *Calf Raises:* 10 repetitions
- *Wrist Flexion & Extension:* 5 repetitions
- *Body Weight Squats:* 12 repetitions
- *Side Shuffle Left and Right:* 10 each direction
- *High Knees:* 20 each

Warm-Up Exercises

Dynamic Leg Swings

- Stand with neutral posture and one hand on a stable object for balance.
- Lift one leg and swing it forward and back through a comfortable range of motion.
- As the joint warms up, increase your range of motion.
- Repeat the same steps, swinging side to side.

Standing Hip Circles

- Stand tall with neutral spine and your core engaged.
- Lift one leg off the ground and bend your knee 90 degrees. Keep your other knee soft, not locked.
- Keep your chest and belly button facing forward. Move your knee away from the midline of your body, and draw an imaginary circle in the air with your knee.
- Perform 10 repetitions and then switch directions.
- Switch legs and repeat.

Torso Rotations

- Stand with neutral posture and hands at your sides. Bend at the elbow 90 degrees with your hands in fists in front of you.

- Engage your stomach muscles by drawing your navel in.

- Twist left and right at your waist and go through a comfortable range of motion.

- As you feel your muscles warm up, you can increase your range of motion.

Dynamic Side Bends

- Stand tall with your feet shoulder width apart, neutral spine, and your core engaged.

- Reach both arms overhead and lace your fingertips together with your elbows fairly straight and your palms facing the floor.

- Keep your weight evenly distributed between your right and left feet. Bend your upper body to the left and right (side bend).

- Stay in motion, but hold the end range for about 1–3 seconds.

Shoulder Circles

- Stand with neutral posture with your hands at your sides.

- Lift both arms out to a *T* with your palms facing forward.

- Circle your shoulders through their entire range of motion at a comfortable pace.

- Pay close attention to keeping your neck and trapezius relaxed. Use them to stabilize your shoulders, but don't flex them or scrunch them up.

- To get maximum benefit from this movement, keep your torso still and avoid twisting.

Calf Raises

- Stand with neutral posture with your hands at your sides.
- Shift your body weight onto the balls of your feet and lift your heels off the ground as high as you can.
- Hold for 1–3 seconds.
- You can also do this exercise one foot at a time.

Wrist Flexion & Extension

- Kneel or stand tall with your feet shoulder width apart, neutral spine, and your core engaged.
- Hold your arms at your sides, bend your elbows 90 degrees, and make a fist with each hand.
- With your palms up, flex your wrist by bringing the back of your hand toward the top of your forearm. Hold the flexion for 5 seconds.
- Return to neutral wrist and without stopping, bring the inside of your palm toward the bottom of your forearm. Hold the flexion for 5 seconds.

Body Weight Squats

- Stand with neutral posture with your hands at your sides. Have a chair or table nearby in case you need help with balance.
- Place your feet shoulder with apart and point your toes slightly away from one another.

- With 60 percent of your body weight in your heels and your core strong, simultaneously bend your knees and move your bottom toward the back of the room. It should feel like you are going to sit on a chair that is slightly too far away.

- Go as low as you can without pain, or until your thighs are parallel to the floor.

- Keep your knees even with or behind your toes. Your eyes and chest should face forward and slightly down.

Side Shuffle Left and Right

- Stand with athletic posture.

- Shuffle two steps to the right and two steps to the left.

- Start slowly and move laterally left and right 10–20 times in each direction. Build speed as you warm up.

High Knees

- Standing in neutral posture, engage your core by drawing your navel in.

- Focus on a spot on the wall or floor.

- Maintain neutral posture and lift your right leg off the ground, with your knee in front of you, until your thigh is parallel to the floor.

- Hold for 10 seconds, and quickly place your leg back on the floor, transitioning swiftly to lifting your left leg with that thigh parallel to the floor. Hold for 10 seconds.

- As you improve your balance, you will be able to transition quicker between legs. For increased challenge, hold your elevated leg for less time, and focus on transitioning quickly between each leg.

Take-Home Points

1. Before any physical activity—including pickleball—your body needs time to warm up. Routinely skipping warm-ups will increase the likelihood of injury.

2. Dedicating time and effort to warming up will help you play well from the start.

3. Foam rolling, both before and after exercise, can help increase blood flow to allow you to recover.

16

Postgame
Stretch Routine

SANJAY: Does walking to my car after the game count as a cooldown? Is that enough to get my heart rate down? How much can a postgame routine really do for you, anyway?

JES: Sure, you can go sit in a car right after you play while your muscles are cooling down . . . if you want to be stuck in the shape of a chair the rest of your life! I'm kidding—sort of. It's not a must to stretch for a lengthy amount of time right after playing, but it's a fantastic time to do it. You're already warm, so what better time to stretch? **Ten minutes** is great, and more is OK too.

Any of the passive stretches in this section will work well in a postpickleball stretch routine. And combining those stretches with foam rolling is a great way to mitigate the effects of a long day of pickleball. Try the full combination of these exercises, or choose your favorites. Descriptions and photos of each exercise are also included here. For a video guide and further info, visit https://pickleballbody.com/videos.

8-Minute Cooldown Stretches

- *Standing Quads Stretch:* 45 seconds each leg
- *Downward-Facing Dog:* 60 seconds
- *Kneeling Reach-Over Stretch:* 45 seconds each side
- *Snow Angel on Foam Roller:* 60 seconds
- *Foam Roller Calf Roll:* 60 seconds each leg

Standing Quads Stretch

- Stand with neutral posture and place one hand on a stable source of support.

- Lift one leg slightly off the ground.

- With your hand, grab your lifted foot and bring it up behind you, as if to kick yourself in the bottom.

- Hold this position for 45 seconds and switch legs.

- If you cannot reach your foot with your hand, use a stretch strap or towel to perform the stretch.

Downward-Facing Dog

- Start from a straight arm plank.
- Point your tailbone toward the ceiling and walk your feet slightly toward your hands until you feel a stretch down the back of your legs.
- Keeping your knees fairly straight, gently push your chest toward your thighs while allowing your heels to drop slowly toward the floor. Your heels do not have to touch the ground.

Kneeling Reach-Over Stretch

- Starting on your hands and knees, move your bottom toward your heels while keeping your arms straight.
- With your arms straight out in front of you, you should start to feel a stretch along the sides of your back.

- Move both hands slightly to your right, across the midline of your body. Side bend ever so slightly to feel a stretch on the opposite side.

- Repeat, reaching the other direction.

Snow Angel on Foam Roller (also see Appendix)

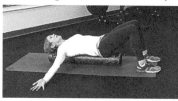

- Using a foam roller, lie down lengthwise directly on the roller with your bottom at one end, head at the other, and spine directly over the roller.

- Place your arms out to your sides, making a *T* with your palms up.

- Keeping your arms fairly straight, slowly arch your arms over your head, stopping at brief intervals to feel the stretch.

Foam Roll Calves (also see Appendix)

- You will need a foam roller for this exercise.
- Sitting on the floor, place your right leg on the roller above your ankle.
- Keep your calf relaxed. Your foot should be dangling. Lift your bottom off the ground and roll from above your ankle to below your knee, the length of your calf.
- Repeat 3 times.
- Staying on the same leg and relaxing your calf, rotate your knee and toes inward toward the midline of your body. Roll the inner portion of your calf 3 times.

- On the same leg, with a relaxed calf, rotate your knee and toes away from the midline of your body. Roll the outer portion of the length of your calf 3 times.

- Switch legs and repeat.

Take-Home Points

1. Aim to stretch and foam roll for 5–10 minutes postworkout.
2. Combine static stretching with foam rolling to best restore blood flow to tired muscles.

17

Sanjay's Pickleball Equipment Cabinet

JES: Sanjay, you're an avid pickleballer and have an assortment of things to help you avoid the aches and pains of regular playing. Can you share what items you have in your pickleball cabinet?

SANJAY: Happy to, Jes! Since picking up the pickleball paddle nearly four years ago, you have helped me perform and recover well through many of the exercises we've already discussed. Over time—and with your guidance—I've collected an assortment of equipment that supplements my training. These items help me on the court or reduce aches after playing. Some people will have many of these items already, but some may be new—and can help others like they have helped me.

I regularly use the following items to remain healthy while playing pickleball. You can find them on Amazon or at Target, Walmart, or your local sporting goods store. Depending on how long or strenuous the level of play is, I may utilize some or all when I step on or off the court. The brands listed in this chapter are simply my personal preferences, and images are included for items that may be helpful to see. I have not tried a variety of brands for all items, and I have no paid endorsements for these products—I'm not *that* good at pickleball . . . yet. ☺ So feel free to use this as a rough guide. For a video on how to use some of the items below, such as the Theragun and more, visit https://pickleballbody.com/videos.

Given my background as a physician, I'll walk through this using a systematic, head-to-toe approach. Essentially, your head, shoulders, knees, and toes (as the children's song goes).

Head

First, a **hat**. You may have heard the saying, "If people are not laughing at your hat, it's not big enough." They are correct. Besides keeping the sun out of your eyes for better visibility on an outdoor court, a large-brim hat is essential for protecting your skin from harsh UV rays. I have found that the Tilley Endurables lighter-weight mesh hat works best. The mesh sides  of the hat keep you cool while you play, while the adjustable under-the-chin drawstring ensures it won't fall off during quick movements. Also, the brim is wide enough to guard your skin down to your neck with UPF 50+ protection. Best of all, it is easy to wash (just throw it in the washer with other items, and let it dry on a hook). If I'm on the court, this hat is on my head!

Next, **sunscreen**. Assuming you are playing outside, sunscreen is a must. Any exposed skin ought to be covered to prevent sun damage. My dermatology colleagues recommend SPF 50 or higher. But the best sunscreen is one that you will actually use, so find a type that you enjoy and like. Use a sunscreen that works for your skin type—whether oily, sensitive, or dry—and that has a feel or scent that you prefer, so that you will use it consistently. Remember, sunburn-causing UV rays are still present on cloudy or cool days.

Eye protection. As Jes and I discussed earlier, I was surprised to find that eye injuries are common among pickle-ballers! Eye injury can greatly reduce one's quality of life.[1] Pickleball-related eye injuries are also typically preventable. If you do not already wear prescription eyeglasses, as I do, use athletic eyewear. These often have wide or large frames for full side-to-side visibility and protection. An adjustable strap can keep the eyewear from moving during play.

Arms & Upper Body

Theraband FlexBar. If you experience elbow pain due to repetitive motion (also known as "tennis elbow"), this is for you. The repetitive motion of swinging a racket may overload and inflame the tendons in your elbow.

The Theraband FlexBar contracts your muscles and tendons together. This strengthens the surrounding muscles and makes bending and twisting easier and less painful. The bars come in a variety of colors, indicating various resistance levels. It is recommended that most individuals start with red and work their way up.

To use the bar, grab each end as if holding on to bike handles. Extend your arms out in front of you and twist, as if wringing out a towel as tightly as is comfortable. Slowly untwist to release your muscles, repeating 15 times, twisting each direction. Follow the product instructions when using, and/or watch YouTube videos that demonstrate how to use it. A brief demonstration can be found at https://pickleballbody .com/videos.

Tennis elbow brace. This thin compression brace is worn just a few inches below the elbow to increase circulation, protect tendons from further strain, and relieve pain and inflammation. Wear this while playing if you experience tennis elbow, arthritis, or

tendonitis. One size fits most, and the cushioned strap makes it comfortable to wear hours at a time. I use the Bodyprox brand elbow strap, but many brands are available.

Theragun. The Theragun is one of my favorite pieces of equipment, as it has a multitude of uses. While it is pricier than most items on this list, it has benefits for your entire body. It's also easy to pack for tournaments. A Theragun is essentially a massaging tool that uses vibration therapy to apply a thumping or quick hammering motion to muscles. This massaging of the muscles increases blood flow and helps reduce soreness. While it can be used for many muscles head to toe, my favorite areas to use it are on my forearms, the inside of my elbow, my hamstrings, and the bottoms of my feet. I use this item daily to reduce soreness.

To use the Theragun, simply turn the device on before placing it near the muscle. Move the Theragun across the intended muscle back and forth for 10 seconds at a time, repeating up to three times. Various models have different attachment heads or speeds for a lighter or tougher massage, depending on your needs.

Foam roller. The Gaiam Essentials 36-inch black foam roller is ideal for use on your back and IT band. This firm roller is an excellent way to loosen muscles before play or to massage pains after play. The 36-inch roller is recommended for full-body rolling.

To use it, lie down on your back with your knees bent and your feet flat on the floor. Place the roller under your lower back, and roll back and forth to massage the muscles. To massage your upper back, lift your head as if you are ready to do a sit-up. Place the foam roller under your upper back and roll. See Jes's foam rolling guide in the Appendix for more tips.

Legs

Rumble Roller. The compact Rumble Roller is a textured roller that increases blood flow and relieves soreness from muscles. Similar in looks and application to the smooth foam roller previously mentioned, the Rumble Roller  bumps provide deeper muscle penetration for a more aggressive massage. This is ideal for hamstrings, calves, and larger muscles.

Roll the Rumble Roller along your hamstrings and calves before playing to increase blood flow and afterward to relieve tension. Jes speaks more on how to select and apply a foam roller in the Appendix.

Stretch-out strap. This woven nylon band is meant to aid you in stretching to achieve a deeper, more effective stretch. It's useful for warming up and loosening muscles before and after play.

If you're not flexible, the stretch-out strap comes in handy. For example, I cannot touch my toes when sitting down with my legs straight. Using the stretch-out strap, I simply place the strap across my foot, keeping the band in each hand. I lean forward as if to touch my toes, pulling gently on the band to lean myself closer to my toes. Since I can't reach my toes on my own, the strap gives me something to grab onto. But be careful! Pull too hard and you may injure yourself. This item is meant to be an aid, providing only a slightly deeper stretch than you can do on your own.

Calf-stretching incline board or block. I use the Fit Viva slant board, but many foam or wooden incline blocks will do the trick. This item works a variety of lower leg muscles with one simple motion. Using the incline board promotes ankle stability and mobility while strengthening the calf muscles and muscles surrounding your Achilles tendon. You can do this exercise with-

out weights or while holding weights for increased difficulty.

To use this item, simply stand on the incline board with your toes elevated higher than your heels. Raise your heels as high as possible, standing on your toes. Repeat until you feel a burn in your calves, roughly 15–30 times. The Fit Viva slant board is my personal preference, as you can adjust the level of incline. For increased incline and a better workout as you grow stronger, look for equipment that is adjustable.

Feet

Massage ball with spikes. This small, palm-sized ball is spiked or bumpy in texture. Similar to the Rumble Roller, the textured exterior provides a deep tissue massage, ideal for working out pains and knots. The small spherical shape makes it the perfect tool for rolling in every direction on the ball and arch of your foot. If you struggle with plantar fasciitis, this is a useful tool for relieving pain. It's also small enough to toss in your bag and take with you to use between games on those long tournament days.

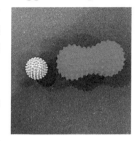

The aptly named peanut massage ball is essentially two spiked massage balls joined together, creating a peanut shape. The peanut massage ball can be useful for a deeper massage on the sides of your foot. But beware: if someone hears you talking about a peanut ball and a pickleball, they might not know you are actually talking about a sport!

My favorite way to use the massage ball is to set it on the ground and put my foot on top, resting the ball of my foot on the top of the ball. Applying pressure as is comfortable, I slowly roll my foot forward and back for 30 seconds at a time. Then I switch to rolling in a circular motion. Do this with each foot about three times. If you would like greater stability, hold a chair or sturdy object for balance.

Next, **shoes**! This one may seem obvious, but supportive shoes play a large role in your level of comfort on the court. I suggest getting new shoes often, as even the best shoes wear down and lose their support over time. Depending on your specific needs, **orthopedic inserts** may be

useful. These correct the way you stand, walk, or run. You can find general supportive inserts in your nearest running shoe store. If you have a condition such as plantar fasciitis, prescription inserts may be necessary. Speak with your personal doctor to find out if they're right for you.

Oofos recovery sandals are what I wear when I am heading to or from the pickleball court. These easy slide-on sandals are so comfortable, I wish I could wear them when I play! I find that wearing comfortable shoes in the hours after pickleball is almost as important as wearing shoes that  help you avoid pain while playing. Oofos are made to help you recover by reducing the stress on your feet, joints, and back with their cradled footbed design and arch support.

Compression socks or sleeves for your forefoot. The SB Sox foot compression sleeve has worked well for me to minimize plantar fasciitis–related pain and boost recovery after play. The compression sleeve protects my ankle through the ball of my foot, providing  stabilization and increased blood flow. The compression sock can provide relief from plantar fasciitis, Achilles pain, arthritis, arch pain, ankle soreness, or swelling after play. I prefer the sleeve form as it focuses on my area of need and doesn't squeeze my toes. But the sleeve or the full sock can provide the support you need.

Lastly, **the tube sock**. ☺ The Thorlos tube sock has been my trusted companion since my basketball days. I suppose Jes is right that these won't fix it all. But I believe a thick, quality tube sock provides comfort and support when standing for several hours on the court. We'll let you decide for yourself!

Take-Home Points

1. Pickleball is a relatively inexpensive game to play, yet it still requires some equipment beyond just a paddle.

2. There are several items one of us has found useful to prevent injuries or to recover quickly after playing—we share these suggestions with all of you.

3. Sanjay's list items are not meant to be firm recommendations—just what he uses before, during, or after playing pickleball. Find the items that work best for you.

Appendix
Foam Rolling Guide

If you are anything like me, you want to stay athletic and fit year after year. In our 20s, avoiding injury barely crossed our minds. Even jumping off a roof somehow seemed doable with minimal risk involved. Almost nothing hurt us. All we had to do was figure out a creative dive roll landing, and we would walk away unscathed!

At this point, maybe you've said good-bye to 20, 30, 40, 50, or 60. You've probably learned through trial and error that your days of physical invincibility bordering on reck-lessness are over. This is why implementing strategies to remain flexible, mobile, and injury-free is just as important as playing pickleball and working out. With these strate-gies, you can continue to compete, challenge yourself, and stay active.

The foam roller is a great tool for improving your mobility and reducing your risk of injury. It's also something you can easily learn to use on your own. This device is a foam cylinder (think pool noodle, but shorter and denser) that allows you to use your own body weight to apply pressure to trigger points and sore, knotted muscles. It's inexpensive, versatile, and portable. The roller comes in a variety of forms: long, short, bumpy, soft, hard, and super hard.

Why Use a Foam Roller?

There is some debate about what the foam roller actually does. Current theories include relaxing the nervous system and breaking up knots and adhesions in and releasing the fascia (the tough tissue that surrounds and connects muscles and tendons). Foam rolling is a great complement to passive stretching. It improves circulation to the targeted area, increasing blood flow to muscles after a workout or a day of pickleball. These things help the recovery process. I suspect there are benefits beyond these, but I must wait for the research to prove me right.

What Is the Difference between Foam Rolling and Stretching?

Stretching releases tension in the muscle tissue by lengthening, while foam rolling applies downward pressure directly into the tissue to release knots and improve blood flow. This allows the tissue to better repair itself.

Using a Foam Roller

- Choose the area you want to roll, and apply moderate pressure using the roller and your body weight.
- Roll slowly—no more than one inch per second.

- You can roll the entire length of the muscle or roll a few inches at a time. You might find that rolling smaller areas provides more relief.

- When you find areas that are tight or painful, pause for several seconds and relax as much as possible. You should slowly start to feel the muscle releasing. After a few seconds, the discomfort or pain should lessen.

- If an area is too painful to apply direct pressure, shift the roller and apply pressure on the surrounding area. Gradually work to loosen the entire area.

- Maintain proper core tightness (navel drawn in) while rolling. This provides crucial stability to the lower back and hips during rolling.

Choosing a Roller

This sounds odd, I know, but choosing the right roller is often based on the amount of pain you feel during use. If the pain is excruciating, you need a softer and possibly smaller roller. If you feel nothing at all, then you should choose a roller that is denser and firmer. If you're competing at high levels, you might need a bumpy roller so you can really dig in.

Foam Rolling Exercises

Here is a list of useful foam rolling exercises to target specific muscles and/or body areas.

Snow Angel

- Using a foam roller, lie down lengthwise directly on the roller with your bottom at one end, head at the other, and spine directly over the roller.

- Place your arms out to your sides, making a *T* with your palms up.

- Keeping your arms fairly straight, slowly arch your arms over your head, stopping at brief intervals to feel the stretch.

Upper Back Roll Out

- Lie down with the foam roller perpendicular to your spine and between your shoulder blades. Keep your knees bent and feet flat on the floor.

- Cross your arms over your chest to create space between the shoulder blades.

- While maintaining a strong core, lift your hips off the ground and roll from below your neck to above your waist. Keep your head in a neutral position.

- After 3–5 passes, change your arm position from across your chest to behind your head so your shoulder blades are close together.

- Perform another 3–5 passes without pulling on your head or neck, keeping your elbows wide apart.

Tensor Fasciae Latae (TFL) & Iliotibial (IT) Band Roll

- Targeting the TFL can be a little tricky, and rolling the IT band can be painful. You can take it in sections if needed.

- Lie face down with your right hip on the roller, and turn your body about 45–60 degrees to your left, shifting your body weight onto the front right side of your hip. (Imagine where your jeans pocket would be on the right side of your body.)

- Roll about 5 passes, about 6 inches in length, while trying to relax the area.

- Now rotate fully onto your right side and roll a vertical section about 6 inches long from the top of your hip bone down.

- When you transition to the IT band, it gets more painful. You don't have to roll it. You can stretch it if you prefer. If rolling, make sure your right leg is raised slightly off the floor and your knee is straight. Maintain your head in neutral, with your ears aligned above your shoulders. Roll the length of your thigh, stopping just above the knee.

Glute

- Sitting on the floor, place your right leg on the roller just below your gluteal fold (where your bottom meets your thigh).

- Keeping your right leg straight and right glute relaxed, roll vertically along your glute.

- After about 5 passes, stop and cross your right leg over your left. Your right ankle will be resting on your left knee. Support your body weight with your right hand.
- Let your right knee open away from your midline, and roll the right glute.

Hamstring

- Sitting on the floor, place your right leg on the roller above your knee.
- Support yourself with your arms as you roll from your knee toward your posterior hip.
- If you are having trouble feeling the roller, try tightening your quadriceps. This should help you relax your hamstrings.
- You can cross one foot over the other to increase leverage.

Quadriceps

- Lie face down with the roller at the top of your right hip. The roller should be placed between the ground and your body. Rest your upper body on your forearms and elbows.
- Keep your quads as relaxed as possible and your toes pointing straight down. Use your arms and left leg to roll the roller down the length of your thigh, stopping just above your knee.
- Repeat 3–5 times, stopping on any tight spots and relaxing the muscles around the tight areas.

- Turn your knee and toes outward away from the midline of your body and roll 3–5 times.
- Move the roller to just above your knee. Turn your knee and toes inward toward the midline of your body and roll the inner, lower two-thirds of your quadriceps.

Calf

- Sitting on the floor, place your right leg on the roller above your ankle.
- Keep your calf relaxed. Your foot should be dangling. Lift your bottom off the ground and roll from above your ankle to below your knee, the length of your calf.
- Repeat 3 times.
- Staying on the same leg and relaxing your calf, rotate your knee and toes inward toward the midline of your body. Roll the inner portion of your calf 3 times.
- On the same leg, with a relaxed calf, rotate your knee and toes away from the midline of your body. Roll the outer portion of the length of your calf 3 times.
- Switch legs and repeat.

References

Chapter 1: Introduction

1. Fleming K. Pickleball mania leading to an epidemic of injuries among baby boomers. *New York Post*. March 1, 2022. https://nypost.com/2022/03/01/pickleball-injuries-are-on-the-rise-amongst-seniors-baby-boomers/. Accessed July 13, 2022.
2. Mortenson P. Who plays pickleball? *Pickleball Magazine*. September/October 2021:9.
3. Coyne C. How pickleball won over everyone from Leonardo DiCaprio to your grandparents. *Vanity Fair*. November 2021: 39A–B. https://archive.vanityfair.com/article/2021/11/01/pickleball-for-all. Accessed October 6, 2022.
4. Florsheim L. Brené Brown on why good leadership has nothing to do with your salary. *WSJ Magazine*. 2021. https://www.wsj.com/articles/brene-brown-on-why-good-leadership-has-nothing-to-do-with-your-salary-11618230703. Accessed July 13, 2022.
5. Larson S. Can pickleball save America? *New Yorker*. July 18, 2022. https://www.newyorker.com/magazine/2022/07/25/can-pickleball-save-america. Accessed October 6, 2022.
6. USA Pickleball. History of the game. https://usapickleball.org/what-is-pickleball/history-of-the-game/. Accessed July 22, 2022.
7. Dwyer K. Pickleball began on Bainbridge Island in 1965 as a summertime diversion for bored kids and since has ballooned

into a full-fledged sport for all ages. *Seattle Times*. 2020. https://www.seattletimes.com/pacific-nw-magazine/sept-20-pickleball/. Accessed July 22, 2022.

8. USA Pickleball. Home. https://usapickleball.org/. Accessed July 13, 2022.

9. USA Pickleball. USA pickleball membership. 2021. https://usapickleball.org/news/membership/. Accessed July 22, 2022.

10. USA Pickleball. 2022 pickleball fact sheet. 2022. https://usapickleball.org/wp-content/uploads/2021/08/2022-Pickleball-Fact-Sheet-updated-5.5.22.pdf. Accessed July 22, 2022.

11. Murphy J. A tennis purist who became a pickleball pro; Why a cardiologist who'd played the traditional racket sport for decades switched to the low-impact alternative with the goofy name. *Wall Street Journal*. January 19, 2019. https://www.wsj.com/articles/a-tennis-purist-who-became-a-pickleball-pro-11547899200. Accessed October 6, 2022.

Chapter 2: Finding Joy in Pickleball

1. USA Pickleball. Pickleball is the fastest-growing sport for second year in a row, growing by 39.3 percent. 2022. https://usapickleball.org/news/fastest-growing-sport/. Accessed July 18, 2022.

2. Gleeson S. Pickleball, the country's fastest growing sport, is also popular in this jail. *USA Today*. 2018. https://www.usatoday.com/story/sports/2018/06/27/pickleball-countrys-fastest-growing-sport-also-popular-cook-county-jail/718232002/. Accessed July 19, 2022.

3. Simon R. Bringing change to the prison system with the power of pickleball. InPickleball. https://inpickleball.com/bringing-change-to-the-prison-system-with-the-power-of-pickleball/. Accessed July 19, 2022.

4. Emack N. Why a 72-year-old man started teaching pickleball in prisons. WBUR. 2019. https://www.wbur.org/onlyagame/2019/07/26/pickleball-prison-cook-county. Accessed July 19, 2022.

5. Mindful Staff. Jon Kabat-Zinn: Defining mindfulness. Mindful. 2017. https://www.mindful.org/jon-kabat-zinn-defining-mindfulness/. Accessed August 5, 2022.

6. Gilmartin H, Goyal A, Hamati MC, Mann J, Saint S, Chopra V. Brief mindfulness practices for healthcare providers—a systematic literature review. *Am J Med* 2017;130(10):1219.e1–.e17.

7. Puddicombe A. All it takes is 10 mindful minutes. TED. 2013. https://youtu.be/qzR62JJCMBQ. Accessed July 19, 2022.

8. Gilmartin H, Saint S, Rogers M, et al. Pilot randomised controlled trial to improve hand hygiene through mindful moments. *BMJ Qual Saf* 2018;27(10):799.

9. Kiken LG, Lundberg KB, Fredrickson BL. Being present and enjoying it: Dispositional mindfulness and savoring the moment are distinct, interactive predictors of positive emotions and psychological health. *Mindfulness (NY)* 2017;8(5):1280–90.

10. Joy. In: *Oxford English Dictionary.* 3rd ed. Oxford University Press; 2020. https://quod.lib.umich.edu/cgi/o/oed/oed-idx?type=entry&byte=216699812. Accessed October 6, 2022.

11. Happiness. In: *Oxford English Dictionary.* 3rd ed. Oxford University Press; 2020. https://www.oed.com/viewdictionaryentry/Entry/84070. Accessed October 6, 2022.

12. Holson LM. Are we living in a post-happiness world? *New York Times.* 2019. https://www.nytimes.com/2019/09/28/sunday-review/joy-happiness-life.html. Accessed October 6, 2022.

13. Lee IF. *Joyful: The Surprising Power of Ordinary Things to Create Extraordinary Happiness.* New York, NY: Little, Brown Spark; 2018.

14. Lama D, Tutu D, Abrams DC. *The Book of Joy: Lasting Happiness in a Changing World.* New York, NY: Avery; 2016; 31, 266.

15. Hanson R. *Hardwiring Happiness: The New Brain Science of Contentment, Calm, and Confidence.* New York, NY: Harmony; 2016.

16. Bernstein E. Why being kind helps you, too—especially now. *Wall Street Journal.* August 12, 2020. https://www.wsj.com/articles/why-being-kind-helps-you-tooespecially-now-11597194000. Accessed October 6, 2022.

17. Pink DH. *Drive: The Surprising Truth about What Motivates Us.* New York, NY: Riverhead; 2011:145.

18. Pérez-Peña R. Graduates cautioned: Don't shut out opposing views. *New York Times.* 2014. https://www.nytimes.com/2014/06/15/us/2014-commencement-speakers.html. Accessed July 19, 2022.

Chapter 4: Wellness Habits for Longevity

1. Wein H. Understanding health risks: Improve your chances for good health. NIH News in Health. 2016. https://newsinhealth.nih.gov/2016/10/understanding-health-risks. Accessed October 2, 2022.

2. 6 numbers you absolutely need to know. Harvard Women's Health Watch. 2013. https://www.health.harvard.edu/staying-healthy/6-numbers-you-absolutely-need-to-know. Accessed October 2, 2022.

Chapter 6: Nutrition 101

1. How much sugar is too much? American Heart Association. https://www.heart.org/en/healthy-living/healthy-eating/eat-smart/sugar/how-much-sugar-is-too-much. Accessed July 20, 2022.

2. Water: How much should you drink every day? Mayo Clinic. 2020. https://www.mayoclinic.org/healthy-lifestyle/nutrition

-and-healthy-eating/in-depth/water/art-20044256#:~:text
=The%20U.S.%20National%20Academies%20of,fluids%20a
%20day%20for%20women. Accessed July 20, 2022.

3. Chart of high-fiber foods. Mayo Clinic. 2021. https://www
.mayoclinic.org/healthy-lifestyle/nutrition-and-healthy
-eating/in-depth/high-fiber-foods/art-20050948. Accessed
July 20, 2022.

Chapter 7: Core & Posture

1. Reid T, Walker J, Hamilton W. *Essays on the Intellectual Powers of Man*. Cambridge, MA: J. Bartlett; 1850.

Chapter 8: Mobility & Flexibility

1. Lee B. *The Tao of Gung Fu: A Study in the Way of Chinese Martial Art*. North Clarendon, VT: Tuttle; 2015.

2. Flexibility. In: *Medical Dictionary for the Health Professions and Nursing*. Farlex; 2012. https://medical-dictionary.thefreedictionary.com/flexibility. Accessed October 6, 2022.

3. Mobility. In: *Miller-Keane Encyclopedia and Dictionary of Medicine, Nursing, and Allied Health*. 7th ed. 2003. https://medical-dictionary.thefreedictionary.com/mobility. Accessed October 6, 2022.

Chapter 9: Balance, Coordination & Agility

1. Balance. In: *The Random House Unabridged Dictionary*. Random House; 2022. https://www.dictionary.com/browse/balance. Accessed October 6, 2022.

2. Coordination. In: LEXICO. Oxford Languages; 2022. https://tinyurl.com/yrc8e9ty. Accessed October 6, 2022.

3. Agility. In: *The Random House Unabridged Dictionary*. Random House; 2022. https://www.dictionary.com/browse/agility. Accessed October 6, 2022.

Part 3: Prevent & Manage Injuries

1. Rubin DI. Epidemiology and risk factors for spine pain. *Neurol Clin* 2007;25(2):353–71.

Chapter 11: Improving Hip Mobility & Preventing Lower Back Problems

1. Rubin DI. Epidemiology and risk factors for spine pain. *Neurol Clin* 2007;25(2):353–71.

Chapter 17: Sanjay's Pickleball Equipment Cabinet

1. Assi L, Chamseddine F, Ibrahim P, et al. A global assessment of eye health and quality of life: a systematic review of systematic reviews. *JAMA Ophthalmol* 2021;139(5):526–41.

Index

Page numbers in *italics* refer to figures.

Achilles tendon, *176*, 178, 230, 232
   exercises, 179–85
agility, 102–3, 105–6
   exercises, 107–13
alcohol, 35
Alternating Single Leg Knee-to-Chest Tucks, 191, *191*
Ankle Circles, 96, *96. See also* Seated Ankle Circles
ankles, 91, 162, 178, 232
   exercises, 96, 179–85
Antirotation, 80–81, *80*
arthritis, 167, 227, 232
awareness, 32–33

back, 61, 62–65, 74, *142*, 238
balance, 33, 74, 75, 102–4, 106
   dynamic, 104
   exercises, 91–101, 107–13, 188–94
   intermediate, 192–94
   static, 104
Ball of Foot Push Offs, 173–74, *173*

Bilateral Turtle, 154, *154*
Body Weight Squats, 214–15, *214*
Bridge Heel Walk Outs, 172, *172*

Calf Raises, 171, *171*, 213, *213*
calf-stretching incline board or block, 230, *230*
calves, *176*, 178
   exercises, 171, 213, 222–23, 241
   stretches, 94–95, 179–85
Cat/Cow/Table, 70–71, *70*, 126–27, *126*
center of gravity, 104
Chest Clasp Stretch, 69–70, *69*, 124–25, *124*
Chin to Clavicle Stretch, 130–31, *130*
community, 44
compression socks or sleeves, 232–33, *232*
consistency, 26, 33–34
cooldown, 218–23

coordination, 102–3, 104–5, 106
  exercises, 107–13, 188–94,
    195–96
core, 61, 71–81, 73, 143, 151–58
  definition, 72
  exercises, 76–81, 152
C posture. *See* forward slump
  posture

dairy products and substitutes,
  54
diet, 41–42, 46–50. *See also*
  foods; nutrition
Double Chin, 68–69, *68*, 131,
  131
Downward-Facing Dog, 99, *99*,
  149, *149*, 220, *220*
Drinking Bird, 193, *193*
Dynamic Leg Swings, 208, *208*
Dynamic Side Bends, 211, *211*

Ear to Shoulder Stretch,
  129–30, *129*
"eat lean" plan, 52–54
elbows, 123, 226
  exercises, 137–39
equipment, 224–33
exercise plans, 42–43
exercises
  Achilles tendon, 179–85
  agility, 107–13
  ankle, 96, 179–85, *182*
  balance, 91–101, 107–13,
    188–94

calf, 171, 213, 222–23, 241
coordination, 107–13, 195–96
core, 76–81, 152
elbow, 137–39
feet, 172–74, 183–84
flexibility, 91–101
glutes, 157, 239–40
hamstring, 162–67, 169–70,
  240
hip, 97, 143–47, 194, 209
IT band, 162
knee, 111, 168–74, 216
leg, 208
mobility, 91–101
neck, 129–32
posture, 66–81
quads, 162–67, 240–41
shoulder, 92, 125–26, 133–35
stability, 91–101, 188–94
strength, 162, 168–74
upper body, 123–39
warm-up, 208–16
wrist, 137, 213–14
eye injuries, 187, 226
eye protection, 226

Facedown Quads Stretch,
  99–100, *99*, 151, *151*
falls, 187–88
fats, 42, 53–54
feet, 178, 230–33
  exercises, 172–74, 183–84
fiber, 42, 53
fish, 52, 53

flexibility, 84, 88–90, 122,
143–47
exercises, 91–101
Foam Roll Calves, 181–82, *181*,
222–23, *222*
foam rollers, 67, 124, 181–82,
221–22, 228, *228*, 235–41
Foam Roll Quads, 163, *163*
foods, 52
fat-free, 47
plant-based, 35
whole, 35, 54
See also diet; nutrition
Foot Roll Out, 184, *184*
Forearm Flexion and Extension
Stretch, 136, *136*
Forearm Pronation and
Supination, 139, *139*
Forward Fold IT Band Stretch,
164, *164*
forward slump posture, *63*,
64–65

glutes, 151, *161*
exercises, 157, 239–40
stretches, 147–51
goals, 27–30, 41, 50–52

habits, 26, 33, 35–36
Half-Hip Hinge with Rotation,
194, *194*
Hamstring Ball Curl, 169–70,
169
hamstrings, *161*

exercises, 162–67, 169–70,
240
stretches, 164–66
happiness, 17–21
hats, 225–26, *225*
health history, 36–37
Heel-to-Toe Walk (Forward
and Backward), 192, *192*
High Knees, 111–12, *111*, 216, *216*
hips, 72, 91, *142*, 143, 162
exercises, 97, 143–47, 194,
209
flexibility, 143–47
posture and, 62, 64
stretches, 148–49
history of pickleball, 6–9
hydration, 42, 53

iliotibial (IT) band, *161*
exercises, 162–67
inmates, 12–14
Internal and External Rotation
Lying Down Face Up,
133–34, *133*
IT band. *See* iliotibial (IT) band

joy, 17–20, 26

key health indicators, 37–38,
49
kindness, 20–23
kinetic chain, 74–75
Kneeling Hip Flexor Stretch,
148–49, *148*

Index

Kneeling Reach-Over Stretch,
    70, *70*, 126, *126*, 220–21,
    220
knees, 91, 167–74
    exercises, 111, 168–74, 216

Lean Code, 40–43
legs, 143, 178, 229
    exercises, 208
    stretches, 147–51
lower body, 75
Lower Body Hold, 78–80, *78*,
    155–56, *155*
Lying Down Ts, Ys, Is, 134–35,
    134

massage tools, 227–28,
    230–31, *231*
meat, 52, 53
men's health, 38, 53
mental health, 14–15
mental skills, 32–38, 44
mind-body strategies, 44
mindfulness, 14–16
Miniband Clam Bridge, 158, *158*
Miniband External Rotator
    Activation from Kneeling,
    135, *135*
Miniband Glute Bridge, 157,
    157
mobility, 43–44, 84, 88–89,
    90–91
    ankle, 162, 167
    elbow, 137–39

exercises, 91–101
    hip, 143–47, 167
    neck, 129–32
    shoulder, 133–35
    upper body, 122, 123–39
motivation, 26
Moving Groin Stretch, 98, *98*,
    147–48, *147*

neck, 123
    exercises, 93, 129–32
    muscles, *121*
Neck Mobilization (Left and
    Right), 93, *93*, 132, *132*
neutral posture, 61–64, *63*
neutral spine, 62
nutrition, 42, 47–54. *See also*
    diet; foods
nuts and seeds, 54

oils, 54
Oofos recovery sandals, 232,
    232

pelvis, 62, 72, 91, 151
pivoting, 44
plantar fasciitis, 85–87,
    179–85, 232
portion sizes, 53
postural deviations, 64–65
posture, 61–71, *63*
    exercises, 66–81
poultry, 52, 53
protein, 42, 53

quadriceps (quads), *161*
  exercises, 162–67, 240–41
  stretches, 99–100, 151, 219
Quick Feet, 112, *112*, 195, *195*

Radial and Ulnar Deviation,
    138, *138*
recovery, 43, 44
referred pain, 123
repetitive motion, 122, 226
restoration, 43, 44
rotational movement, 71, 74
Rumble Roller, 229, *229*

Scapula Protraction/Retraction,
    67–68, *67*
Scapula Protraction/Retraction
    from Table Pose, 127–28,
    127
Seated Ankle Circles, 182, *182*
Seated Glute Stretch, 150, *150*
shoes, 231–32, *231*
Shoulder Circles, 92–93, *92*,
    125–26, *125*, 212, *212*
shoulders, 62, 91, 123
  exercises, 92–93, 125–26,
    133–35
  muscles, *121*
  stretches, 129–30
Shuffle–Shuffle Touch, 113, *113*,
    196, *196*
Side Plank, 77–78, *77*
Side Shuffle Left and Right,
    215, *215*

Single Leg Balance with
    Assistance, 108, *108*,
    189–90, *189*
Single Leg Balance without
    Assistance (Eyes Open,
    Eyes Closed), 109, *109*,
    190–91, *190*
Single Leg Balance without
    Assistance (Limbs in
    Motion), 110–11, *110*
sleep, 35
Snow Angel on Foam Roller,
    67, *67*, 124, *124*, 221, *221*
socks, 232–33, *232*
Spiderman Hip Mobility,
    145–46, *146*
spine, 72, 91, 123, 151
Squats Using a Miniband,
    170–71, *170*
stability, 74, 75
  exercises, 91–101
Stair Calf Stretch, 185, *185*
Standing Abduction, 145, *145*
Standing Calf Stretch:
    Gastrocnemius, 94, *94*,
    179–80, *179*
Standing Calf Stretch: Soleus,
    95, *95*, 180–81, *180*
Standing Hamstring Stretch, *165*
Standing Hamstring Stretch:
    Single Leg, 165–66
Standing Hamstring Stretch
    with Hands Behind the
    Back, 164–65, *164*

Standing Hip Circles, 97, *97*, *144*, *144*, 209, *209*
Standing Quads Stretch, 166–67, *166*, 219, *219*
Straight Arm and Forearm Plank, 76–77, *76*, 152–53, *152*
stress, 33, 43, 44
stress hormones, 20
stretches, 69–70
  calf, 94–95, 179–85
  cooldown, 218–22
  glute and upper leg, 147–51
  hamstring, 164–66
  hip, 148–49
  neck, 129–32
  quad, 99–100, 151, 219
  shoulder, 129–30
stretching
  dynamic, 5, 89
  passive, 43, 87, 218, 236
  static, 89
stretch-out strap, 229–30, *229*
sugar, 35, 42, 47, 53
sunscreen, 35, 226
superfoods, 42, 52
swayback posture, 63, 64, 65

tendonitis, 227
tennis elbow, 226
tennis elbow brace, 227, *227*

tensor fasciae latae (TFL), 239
Theraband FlexBar, 226–27, *226*
Theragun, 227–28, *228*
Thoracic Rotation from Table Pose, 100–101, *100*, 128, *128*
time management, 44
Torso Rotations, 210, *210*
Towel Toe Scrunches, 183, *183*
tube socks, 233

upper body, 71, 75
  exercises, 123–39
USA Pickleball Association (USAPA), 8–9

vibration therapy, 227–28

Wall Sit, 168–69, *168*
warm-ups, 5, 205–7
  exercises, 208–16
weight
  gain, 48–49
  healthy, 35
  loss, 46–48, 50–51
women's health, 38, 53
Wrist Flexion and Extension, 137, *137*, 213–14, *213*
wrists, 91, 187
  exercises, 137, 213–14